ADVANTAGE Test Prep 7

Table of Contents

Table of Contents

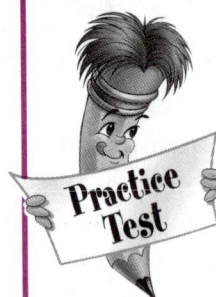

CREDITS

Concept Development: Kent Publishing Services, Inc.

Written by: Jeff Putnam

Design: Moonhee Pak

Production: Signature Design Group, Inc.

Illustrators: Jenny Campbell

Art Director: Tom Cochrane

Project Director: Carolea Williams

Introduction

Testing in reading, writing, language, and mathematics have taken on a large role in education today. This workbook is designed to help students practice the skills and strategies that they will encounter on standardized and proficiency tests. Even if students don't have to take these tests, they will benefit from practicing the skills and strategies taught in this workbook.

Standardized Tests

Standardized tests are administered in the exact same way to hundreds of thousands of students across the United States. They are also referred to as *norm-referenced tests*. Norms give educators a common standard of measurement of students' skills and abilities across the country. Students are ranked according to their test scores and then assigned a percentile ranking. For example, a percentile score of 85 means a student scored higher than 85 percent of the students who also took the same test.

Proficiency Tests

Many states develop their own statewide proficiency tests. Proficiency tests are also known as *criterion-referenced tests*. This means that the test is based on a list of standards and skills (also called criteria). States develop standards for what students should know at each grade level. The proficiency test evaluates a student's mastery of set standards.

Standardized tests and proficiency tests look similar. However, their measurement is different. A proficiency test measures a student's mastery of set standards. A standardized test compares a student's achievement to others who took the same test.

Although the measurement is different, standardized and proficiency tests do have similarities in that they are used to:
- evaluate students' progress, strengths, and weaknesses.
- select students for remedial or achievement programs.
- tell educators where and how school systems can be improved.
- evaluate the success of school programs.
- help educators develop programs to suit their students' specific needs.

Both of these types of achievement tests are administered essentially the same way. They ask multiple-choice and open-response questions, and they have time limits. An important goal of this workbook is to teach test-taking strategies so that no matter which test your child is required to take, he or she will be successful.

Preparing for Tests

The more students are prepared for taking standardized and proficiency tests, the higher they will perform on those tests. A student who understands the skills commonly measured and who practices test-taking strategies is more likely to be a successful test-taker. The more the student knows what to expect, the more comfortable the student will be in the actual test-taking situations.

Many tests were reviewed in developing the material for this workbook. They include the following:

- **California Achievement Tests (CAT)**
- **Comprehensive Test of Basic Skills (CTBS)**
- **TerraNova**
- **Iowa Test of Basic Skills (ITBS)**
- **Metropolitan Achievement Tests (MAT)**
- **Stanford Achievement Tests (SAT)**
- **Texas Assessment of Knowledge and Skills (TAKS)**

It is important to remember that standardized and proficiency tests are only one measure of student achievement. Teachers use many other methods to gain insights into each student's skills, abilities, and knowledge. It is a good idea to speak with your child's teacher to discuss and understand all the methods used in evaluating your child.

Introduction

How Can Parents Help Students Take Standardized Tests Successfully?

The following list includes suggestions on how to help prepare students to do their best on standardized tests.

Tips for Parents
- Monitor your child's progress.
- Get to know your child's teacher; find out what he or she thinks you can do to best help your child at home.
- Be informed about your state's testing requirements.
- Motivate your child to prepare.
- Help your child structure a quiet place and time away from distractions to do homework.
- Read aloud to your child.
- Find learning experiences in everyday life such as making change, reading signs, preparing food, or walking outside.
- Make sure your child is getting the sleep and nutrition he or she needs to succeed.
- Always nurture your child's curiosity and desire to learn.
- Encourage your child to learn about computers and technology.
- Encourage your child to take tests seriously, but to value learning and giving one's best efforts.
- Notice academic efforts your child is making and support and acknowledge what you see.

Where Can I Learn More About Testing?

National Center for Fair and Open Testing, Inc. (FairTest)
342 Broadway
Cambridge, MA 02139
http://www.fairtest.org/

Visit the Web site of the Department of Education for your state. Most states post information about standardized and proficiency tests that they administer to students.

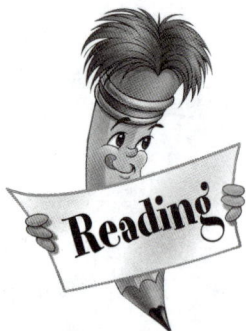

Reading is a skill that will help you do well in school as well as in life. You also need to be a good reader to perform well on standardized tests. The more you read, the better you will read. And the better you read, the more you'll enjoy it and the higher you'll score on tests. Read as much as you can. Choose many different types of reading materials. Read by yourself or with others. Read aloud or silently. Practice listening to how words sound. When you read stories, think about who the characters are and how the story develops and progresses.

Nearly every standardized or proficiency test includes a section on reading. The reading passages may be fiction, nonfiction, or poetry. They may also include graphic information like maps, graphs, charts, or time lines. You might also find reference sources, like indexes or dictionary entries. You will be asked to recall, interpret, and reflect on what you read.

The following pages give a review of reading skills. You will practice the skills with questions just like the ones you will find on standardized tests. Practicing these skills now will help you perform better on test day. In this section, you will learn to:

- use **context** to find the meaning of words.
- examine **roots**, **prefixes**, and **suffixes**.
- analyze **cause and effect**.
- follow **multi-step instructions**.
- make **generalizations**.
- interpret words with **multiple meanings**.
- interpret **analogies**.
- analyze **character**, **plot**, and **conflict**.
- draw **conclusions**.
- analyze literary devices such as **foreshadowing** and **symbolism**.
- make **inferences**.
- read and understand **maps**, **graphs**, **charts**, and **time lines**.
- use an **index**.
- use a **dictionary entry**.

The Science of Flight

If you're like most people, you've probably been puzzled by an odd fact. You know an airplane weighs many tons. Yet, you've looked up in the sky countless times to see one of these amazing (and amazingly heavy) objects flying through the air, seemingly defying gravity. How an airplane—or bird—can stay aloft is a fascinating subject. In fact, the only thing holding the airplane up is air!

The key to flight is a scientific principle called *lift*. It was first described by a Swiss scientist named Daniel Bernoulli in 1738. Lift allows an object to fly, thanks to differences in air pressure. Compare a bird's wing to an airplane's wing and you'll see they share some important characteristics. Both are thicker at the front than at the back. Both are flat on the bottom and curved on the top. Scientists call this unusual shape an *airfoil*.

As Bernoulli discovered, the airfoil shape creates different air pressures above and below the wing. As the bird or airplane moves forward (an activity known as *thrust*) wind rushes over and under the wing. The air rushing over the curved top part has a lower pressure than the air passing underneath the flat bottom of the wing. This pressure difference occurs because faster-moving air has a lower pressure than slower-moving air. The air has to move faster to get over the curved top of the wing than it does to slip by the flat underside.

This difference in air pressure, now known as the Bernoulli effect, actually creates a vacuum. The vacuum pulls the wing upward, along with the rest of the airplane or bird. As long as a wing is moving forward fast enough, the air it meets moves by the wings fast enough to keep the object aloft. Think about what happens when an airplane comes in for a landing. It slows down, resulting in a loss of forward motion, or thrust. Less thrust equals less lift, and the plane drops to the ground.

If you're skeptical that moving air can be powerful enough to lift a heavy object, there's a little experiment you can do. Cut a thin strip of onionskin or tracing paper. Hold the strip of paper just under your lips with both hands. Then blow over the top of the paper. Direct your breath downward over the paper like you're blowing into a pop bottle. You may be surprised at what happens next. As you blow harder, the air coming from your mouth moves faster. However, it doesn't push the paper downward. The slip of paper rises.

You've just experienced the phenomenon that Bernoulli analyzed over 250 years ago. Lift and thrust, the forces that lift your strip of paper, are the same forces that keep jets zooming and birds soaring.

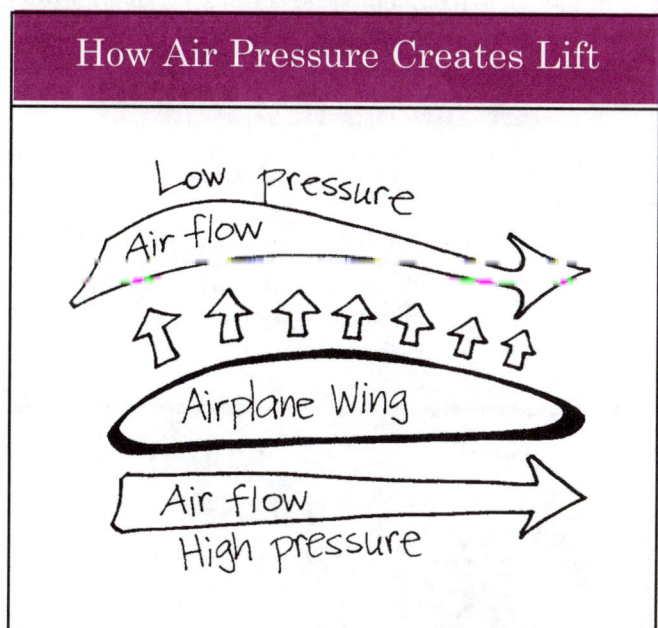

How Air Pressure Creates Lift

Low Pressure
Air flow

Airplane Wing

Air flow
High pressure

VOCABULARY

KNOW THE SKILL: **WORDS IN CONTEXT**

Some test questions ask you to figure out the meaning of a word. Often you can guess the meaning of the word by thinking about the word's context. Context is the meanings of the other words around the unknown word.

DURING THE TEST

To learn what a word means from the context of the sentence, look for the verb or subject in the sentences around it. These words will give you clues about the unknown word.

TEST EXAMPLE

1 Which word means the same thing as *skeptical*?
If you're skeptical that moving air can be powerful enough to lift a heavy object, there's a little experiment you can do.

   (A) certain   (C) unhappy
   (B) doubtful   (D) uninterested

THINK ABOUT THE ANSWER

The correct answer is option B, *doubtful*. Option A is incorrect because if you were certain about the effect of moving air, you wouldn't have to do the experiment. Option C, *unhappy*, doesn't make sense in the sentence. Neither does option D, *uninterested*.

NOW YOU TRY IT

2 Choose the word or words that mean the same thing as *aloft*.

As long as a wing is moving forward fast enough, the air it meets moves by the wings fast enough to keep the object aloft.

   (F) moving
   (G) hanging
   (H) at the front
   (J) in the sky

Check your answer on page 109.

That One's Out

When answering vocabulary questions like these, plug each choice into the sentence and ask yourself if it makes sense. Some will not, and you can eliminate these right away.

Advantage Test Prep Grade 7 © 2005 Creative Teaching Press

Reading

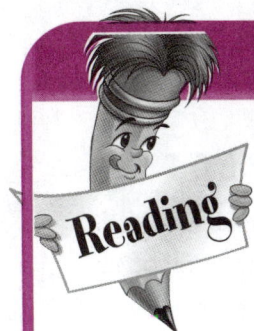

KNOW THE SKILL: ROOTS, PREFIXES, AND SUFFIXES

Tests will ask you to analyze word bases and the beginnings and endings of words to determine word meaning. A **root** is the main part, or base of a word. A **prefix** is placed at the beginning of a root, while a **suffix** goes at the end of a root. Some common prefixes are *un-*, *non-*, *ex-*, *pre-*, and *bi-*. Some common suffixes are *-able*, *-ish*, *-ly*, *-ness*, and *-ance*

DURING THE TEST

Look for a part of an unknown word, the prefix, root, or suffix, that resembles one you already know. For example, *tortuous* contains that same root as *torture*. The adjective suffix *-ous* is added. This helps you guess that the word *tortuous* means, "very hard, almost like being tortured."

TEST EXAMPLE

1. Which word or words best replace *seemingly*?

   An airplane can fly through the air, seemingly defying gravity.

   - Ⓐ as if
   - Ⓑ without
   - Ⓒ proudly
   - Ⓓ in addition to

THINK ABOUT THE ANSWER

The answer is option A. The root *seem* in *seemingly* can mean, "something that looks one way but is really another way." The airplane *seems* to be defying gravity, but as you learn later, it is really held up by the difference in air pressure above and below its wings.

NOW YOU TRY IT

2. Which answer best defines *beneficiaries*?

   Modern business travelers are certainly the beneficiaries of Bernoulli's discoveries.

   - Ⓕ people who study Bernoulli
   - Ⓖ people who ignore Bernoulli
   - Ⓗ people who mistrust Bernoulli
   - Ⓙ people who are positively impacted by Bernoulli

   Check your answer on page 109.

Get Testwise

Beginnings and Endings

Use your knowledge of prefixes and suffixes to eliminate nonsense choices in questions that focus on word meanings.

Reading

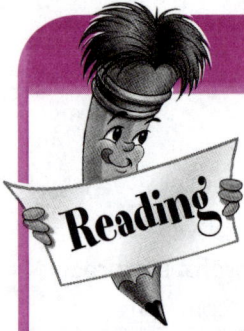

KNOW THE SKILL: ANALYZE CAUSE AND EFFECT

Some test questions will ask you to analyze what caused an event or what the effect of an event was. A **cause** is a reason why something happens. An **effect** is the result of an event or action.

DURING THE TEST

To pinpoint a cause, ask yourself, "What caused this? Why did this event happen?" Find an effect by asking yourself, "What is the result of this? What happened because of this?"

TEST EXAMPLE

1 Choose the answer that best completes the sentence.

As the plane's thrust increased, its lift _____.

Ⓐ decreased slightly
Ⓑ increased the plane's speed
Ⓒ raised the plane from the runway
Ⓓ increased the air pressure below the wings

THINK ABOUT THE ANSWER

Option C is correct. According to the reading selection, the thrust, or forward movement of the plane increases the lift on the wings, allowing the aircraft to take off into the air. The increased thrust is the cause, while the greater lift—and takeoff—is the effect.

NOW YOU TRY IT

2 Choose the answer that best completes the sentence.

Because of Daniel Bernoulli's scientific discoveries about airfoils and air pressure, _____.

Ⓕ birds began to fly.
Ⓖ scientists invented the airfoil.
Ⓗ thrust increased around the world
Ⓙ people were able to develop airplanes

Check your answer on page 109.

Get Testwise

Stay Focused

Do not let anything distract you, especially other test-takers. Don't waste time looking out the window or at the other people in the room. You should have one focus and one focus only—the test!

COMPREHENSION

KNOW THE SKILL: **FOLLOW MULTI-STEP INSTRUCTIONS**

Some tests will ask you to arrange the different steps in a procedure in correct order. You may also be asked to read instructions about a procedure and answer questions about the instructions.

DURING THE TEST

When answering questions about step-by-step procedures or instructions, always ask yourself if the steps are arranged in the most logical order. Check to see whether each step can be done only before or after the other steps.

TEST EXAMPLE

1. Which step is NOT necessary to prove the Bernoulli effect?
   - (A) blowing into a pop bottle
   - (B) cutting a thin strip of paper
   - (C) holding a strip of paper under your lips
   - (D) blowing over the top of a strip of paper

THINK ABOUT THE ANSWER

Option A is the correct answer. Blowing into a pop bottle is not part of the procedure described in the selection. The text says to blow over the thin strip of paper as if you were blowing into a pop bottle.

NOW YOU TRY IT

2. Which step in the procedure described in the selection must be performed first?
   - (F) Blow downward over a strip of paper.
   - (G) Hold a strip of paper under your lips.
   - (H) Cut out a thin strip of paper.
   - (J) Lift up the strip of paper.

Check your answer on page 109.

Write It Down

When working with instructions or procedures, don't hesitate to use scratch paper to make notes about the correct order of the steps.

Reading

KNOW THE SKILL: MAKE GENERALIZATIONS

When you make a generalization, first draw a conclusion based on what you have read in a selection. Base your conclusion on what you read and what you already know. Then, use the conclusion to make a generalization. Go beyond what you have read to make a broader statement that you believe to be true and correct, based on your reading and previous knowledge.

DURING THE TEST

Test a possible answer by saying "In general…" and then the statement. If it sounds wrong or unrelated to the information, eliminate it.

TEST EXAMPLE

1. Which generalization about the selection is the most accurate?
   - (A) Flying is very dangerous.
   - (B) Most people are afraid of flying.
   - (C) Experiments with strips of paper are not very convincing.
   - (D) Successful flight depends on a good understanding of scientific principles.

THINK ABOUT THE ANSWER

The correct answer is option D. It is supported by both the selection and by common knowledge. The other options are not supported by the selection so they can be ruled out.

NOW YOU TRY IT

2. Which generalization is NOT supported by the selection?
   - (F) Air pressure is not very well understood.
   - (G) Modern science builds on the contributions of many people.
   - (H) Many people probably do not understand the science of flight.
   - (J) Experiments can convince people about the truth of scientific ideas.

Check your answer on page 109.

Get Testwise

Build Your Stamina

Some standardized tests can last for hours, so it is important to get use to working for long periods of time. Set aside longer and longer periods of time to do your homework. This will help you stay sharp during a long test.

Daedalus and Icarus

Long ago, there lived a great inventor and architect named Daedalus. He had designed the most wonderful building, a great maze called the *Labyrinth*, for the king of the island nation of Crete. At first Minos, the king, was grateful, but his feelings soon changed. He imprisoned Daedalus, along with his young son Icarus, in a tower on the island. Daedalus and Icarus were downcast. There seemed to be no possible way to escape their island prison.

Then one day, Daedalus was gazing up in the sky. Far above him, he saw birds soaring. What if I made wings for us, he mused, so that we could fly to freedom? The great inventor began immediately to fashion wings from feathers and thread. The massive wings were held together by wax. When the wings were finished, Daedalus fastened them to his arms. With some practice, he learned to use them. When the wind was blowing just right, he was able to soar into the skies. The path to freedom was now clear!

He made a smaller set for Icarus and showed him how to use them. As the boy's skill improved, Daedalus warned him sternly. "You must never fly too low or too high. If you fly too low, the fog will weigh you down," he cautioned in a grave voice. "But if you fly too high, the heat of the blazing sun will melt the wax that holds your wings together." Icarus nodded, but he was an excitable boy.

Then one day, a fresh wind blew up, gusting away from the island. Daedalus knew the moment had come. Carefully, Daedalus put on his wings. Then he helped his son on with his own set. After a final warning to the boy, the two set off. Slowly at first, but gaining speed and altitude, they began to ride the fresh breezes. It took their breath away to see the island far below. Islanders who looked up thought they saw gods soaring through the clear blue sky. Daedalus kept a close watch on the boy, who was beginning to feel a great excitement.

As he soared like a noble eagle, Icarus' heart soared as well. He began to wish for even greater thrills, and he soon forgot his father's stern warning. He swooped low, almost splashing through the rolling waves. Then he climbed, flapping his wings to take him higher and higher. He saw his father flying far ahead and below, but caution was lost in his growing excitement. So delirious with joy was Icarus that he did not notice the air growing warmer.

Suddenly Icarus felt himself slowly falling. He flapped his wings harder, but it was no avail. He watched in horror as the feathers fell from his wings. Faster and faster he plummeted. The doomed boy's last thought as he disappeared under the waves was his father's warning. All that was left for his grief-stricken father to see were a few feathers floating on the water.

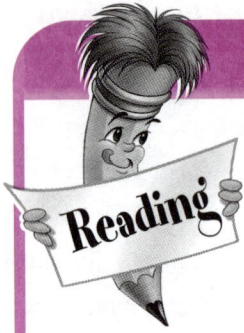

Reading

KNOW THE SKILL: WORDS WITH MULTIPLE MEANINGS

Many words have more than one meaning. Sometimes, the same word can be different parts of speech and be used in different ways in a sentence. Tests may ask you to pick the correct meaning of a word, or choose a word that has the same meaning as one used in a text.

DURING THE TEST

The first step to choosing the correct word or meaning is knowing how it is used in the sentence. Look for clues that will tell you how a word is used. For example, nouns are often modified by adjectives. Verbs have endings like -s, -ed, and -ing and are modified by adverbs that often end in -ly.

TEST EXAMPLE

1 Read the sentence from the story. Choose the meaning of the word *fashion*.

The great inventor began immediately to fashion wings from feathers and thread.

- Ⓐ style
- Ⓑ adapt
- Ⓒ clothing
- Ⓓ construct

THINK ABOUT THE ANSWER

Option D is the correct answer. *Fashion* is a word that can be both a verb and a noun; in this case, it is a verb. You can determine that it is a verb because of its position and use in the sentence. Options A and C can be eliminated because they are not verbs. Option B is a verb that does not make sense in the context of the sentence.

NOW YOU TRY IT

2 Read the sentence from the story. Choose the meaning of *grave*.

"You must never fly too low or too high. If you fly too low, the fog will weigh you down," he cautioned in a grave voice.

- Ⓕ a burial place
- Ⓖ dangerous
- Ⓗ dignified
- Ⓙ serious

Check your answer on page 109.

Get Testwise

Take Another Look

In questions like these, you'll benefit from reviewing the main parts of speech and how they're used in sentences. Knowing the parts of speech will help you identify correct meanings of words that have several possible meanings.

Reading

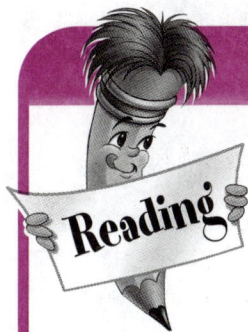

KNOW THE SKILL: INTERPRET ANALOGIES

Analogy questions ask you to find relationships between things. When you understand the relationship between two words, you can select the answer that expresses the same relationship between another set of words.

DURING THE TEST

It helps to know what kind of word you are looking for in your answer. For example, if the word in the first position in the first pair of words is a verb, then you know you have to choose a verb in the second pair. The same goes for nouns, adjectives, and other parts of speech.

TEST EXAMPLE

1 *Delirious* is to *excited* as _____ is to *unhappy*.
- Ⓐ joyous
- Ⓑ confused
- Ⓒ sorrowful
- Ⓓ desperation

THINK ABOUT THE ANSWER

Option C is correct. *Delirious* describes an extreme form of excitement, while *sorrowful* describes an extreme form of unhappiness. Both are adjectives. Option A is incorrect because *joyous* is the opposite of *unhappy*. Option B is incorrect because *confused* is not an extreme form of unhappiness. Option D is incorrect because *desperation* is a noun, not an adjective.

NOW YOU TRY IT

2 *Design* is to *building* as *compose* is to _____.
- Ⓕ create
- Ⓖ bridge
- Ⓗ wonderful
- Ⓙ symphony

Check your answer on page 109.

Grab that Pencil

When working analogies, you may find it helpful to make a little diagram. On one line, write the pair of words you know. On a second line, write the word you are supplied, and leave a blank for the word you need to find. Fill in the blank with the choices offered to see which one fits best.

Reading

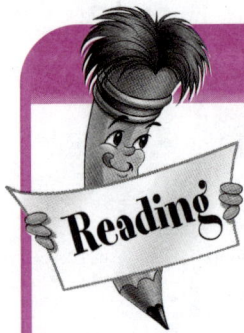

KNOW THE SKILL: ANALYZE CHARACTER

Tests will frequently ask you to analyze characters in a story. One type of question focuses on why characters in stories do what they do. The reason a character in a story makes a particular choice is called **motivation**.

DURING THE TEST

Ask yourself as you read a story why the characters do what they do. What are their reasons for making particular choices? How do you know?

TEST EXAMPLE

1. Which of the following is probably NOT a motivation for why Minos imprisons Daedalus and Icarus on Crete?
   - (A) He wants to keep Daedalus from designing great buildings for other kings.
   - (B) He wants Daedalus to build other buildings for him on Crete.
   - (C) He wants Daedalus to work on new inventions for him alone.
   - (D) He wants to kill Daedalus and Icarus.

THINK ABOUT THE ANSWER

Option D is the correct answer. It is probably not a motivation for Minos because if he wanted to kill Daedalus and Icarus he would not have gone to the trouble of putting them in prison.

NOW YOU TRY IT

2. Which answer best describes Daedalus' motivation for warning Icarus not to fly too high or low?
   - (F) He knew his son was excitable and might be foolhardy.
   - (G) He had seen birds fly too high and too low.
   - (H) He was proud of his son's skill.
   - (J) He was afraid of Minos.

Check your answer on page 109.

Get Testwise

Make a Note
Feel free to make notes in the margins of the test about characters' motivations. Notes can make it easier to quickly find places where the characters' motivations are explained.

Reading

KNOW THE SKILL: ANALYZE PLOT

The events of a story, in the order they happen, are called the **plot**. Tests may ask you to list plot events, place them in the correct order, or analyze them in some way.

DURING THE TEST

To make clear the plot of a story, retell it to yourself using words like *first*, *next*, *then*, and *finally*. These "ordering" words can help you see how the events of the plot fit together. Don't forget that some important plot events could have taken place before the part of the story you are reading is happening.

TEST EXAMPLE

1. Which plot event in the story happened first?
   - A   Icarus flies too close to the sun.
   - B   Daedalus decides to construct wings.
   - C   Daedalus longs to escape from the tower.
   - D   Daedalus and Icarus practice flying with their wings.

THINK ABOUT THE ANSWER

Option C is the correct answer. All the other choices take place after Daedalus gazes at the flying birds and longs to escape. The correct order of the plot events listed as choices is C, B, D, A.

NOW YOU TRY IT

2. Which plot event in the story happened before the story begins?
   - F   Islanders looked up to see the two flying figures.
   - G   Minos imprisons Daedalus and Icarus in the tower.
   - H   Daedalus gazes at the birds soaring above the island.
   - J   Daedalus warns his son about flying too high or too low.

Check your answer on page 109.

Get Testwise

Pick One Answer

Select only one answer for each question. If you fill in two, your answer will be marked wrong.

KNOW THE SKILL: ANALYZE CONFLICT

The events of a story are called the plot. One of the elements in a story that directs events is conflict. **Conflict** is the relationship between different characters, between characters and nature, or even between the different ways characters might feel about themselves. Tests often ask you to analyze conflict in a fiction selection.

DURING THE TEST

A good way to analyze conflict is to ask yourself as you read, "What problems do the characters face? What are they trying to overcome? What prevents them from achieving success?" These and other questions will help you identify and analyze conflict.

TEST EXAMPLE

1   Which answer best describes the conflict between Daedalus and Minos?
   - Ⓐ   Daedalus wants Icarus to escape with him, but Icarus wants to remain with Minos.
   - Ⓑ   Daedalus wants to build another Labyrinth, but Minos has put him in prison.
   - Ⓒ   Daedalus wants to leave the island, but Minos will not let him go.
   - Ⓓ   Daedalus wants to fly safely, but Minos is young and reckless.

THINK ABOUT THE ANSWER

Option C is the correct answer. The conflict between Minos and Daedalus focuses on Daedalus' desire to flee his prison on the island. Minos does not want him to go.

NOW YOU TRY IT

2   Which answer best describes the conflict between Daedalus and Icarus?
   - Ⓕ   Daedalus disobeys Icarus' warnings during their escape from the island.
   - Ⓖ   Icarus does not heed Daedalus' warning about flying too high.
   - Ⓗ   Daedalus and Icarus have different opinions about Minos.
   - Ⓙ   Icarus refuses to learn to fly using the wings.

Check your answer on page 109.

Don't Rely on Your Memory
When answering questions about a reading passage, go back and re-read the passage. Don't rely on your memory. Read the question, then skim selection to find the section where the information is located. Read that section carefully.

KNOW THE SKILL: DRAW CONCLUSIONS

When you draw a conclusion, you figure out something about a story, event, or character that the author did not tell you directly. To draw a conclusion, use information from the selection, combined with your own knowledge and experiences.

DURING THE TEST

Read between the lines. Try to think about the wider meanings behind what the author tells you. For example, if a text describes a foolish character who keeps making the same mistake over and over, a conclusion you might draw is that wise people should try to learn from their errors.

TEST EXAMPLE

1 Which answer is the best conclusion you could draw about the story?
- Ⓐ People should not try to fly like birds.
- Ⓑ Imprisoned people will do foolhardy things.
- Ⓒ Children should follow their parents' advice.
- Ⓓ Making wings from wax and feathers is a bad idea.

THINK ABOUT THE ANSWER

Option C is the correct answer. Icarus should have followed his father's advice; if he had, he would not have met his terrible fate. Options A and D are, in fact, not true, because the escape would have been successful if Icarus had obeyed his father. Option B is not true because Daedalus' plan was sound, not foolhardy.

NOW YOU TRY IT

2 Which of the following is NOT a conclusion you could draw about the story?
- Ⓕ Daedalus did what he could to warn Icarus about the dangers of flying.
- Ⓖ Daedalus was wrong to try to escape from Crete.
- Ⓗ Daedalus was a great inventor.
- Ⓙ Daedalus was a caring father.

Check your answer on page 109.

What's the Reason?

Make sure you can support your answers in questions like these with evidence from the selection. You can't just say you think something—you need to base your responses on evidence from the selection.

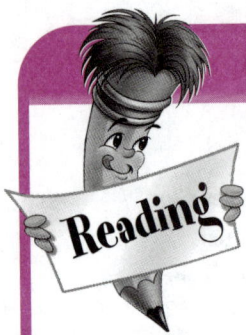

KNOW THE SKILL: **FORESHADOWING**

Writers use literary devices to make their writing more interesting and enjoyable. One of these devices is called foreshadowing. **Foreshadowing** is a kind of hint an author includes earlier in a story to let readers know that something is going to happen later in the story. The selection about Daedalus and Icarus contains several examples of foreshadowing. Tests may ask you to find and explain examples of foreshadowing.

DURING THE TEST

As you read, keep a lookout for sentences that seem as if they are pointing forward to something important that might happen. Sometimes they occur at the end of paragraphs.

TEST EXAMPLE

1 Which sentence from the story is an example of foreshadowing?
- Ⓐ Icarus nodded, but he was an excitable boy.
- Ⓑ At first Minos, the king, was grateful, but his feelings soon changed.
- Ⓒ When the wind was blowing just right, he was able to soar into the skies.
- Ⓓ Slowly at first, but gaining speed and altitude, they began to ride the fresh breezes.

THINK ABOUT THE ANSWER

Option A is the correct answer. The author tells us that, although Icarus understood his father's important advice, he was an excitable boy. This is a clue that, later in the story, something bad may happen to Icarus because of his excitable nature. In fact, it causes his destruction. The other choices do not foreshadow later events.

NOW YOU TRY IT

2 Which sentence from the story is an example of foreshadowing?
- Ⓕ It took their breath away to see the island far below.
- Ⓖ As he soared like a noble eagle, Icarus' heart soared as well.
- Ⓗ There seemed to be no possible way to escape their island prison.
- Ⓙ The great inventor began immediately to fashion wings from feathers and thread.

Check your answer on page 109.

Don't Get Stuck!

Sometimes you'll come across a tricky question. Don't let it worry you. Reread the question, then try to solve it. If you find yourself stumped, circle the question and move on. You can come back to it later. If you still don't know the answer, review your options and make the best guess you can.

Read the poem, *Dreams*. Then complete the activities on pages 22 through 23.

Dreams

by Langston Hughes

Hold fast to dreams
For if dreams die
Life is a broken-winged bird
That cannot fly.

Hold fast to dreams
For when dreams go
Life is a barren field
Frozen with snow.

KNOW THE SKILL: **SYMBOLISM**

A symbol is a person, place, event, or object that has a special meaning apart from what it actually is. For example, a flag is a piece of cloth. But it is also a symbol of a nation and the values the nation honors. In a poem or story, a horse could be a symbol of power or freedom. Not every reading passage contains a symbol, but many do. Tests are likely to ask you about symbols.

DURING THE TEST

As you read a poem or story, look for objects that are repeated or that have a prominent role in the story. Then decide whether the object has a deeper meaning. An author may be using this object as a symbol.

TEST EXAMPLE

1 In the first stanza of the poem, what does the broken-winged bird symbolize?
- Ⓐ a life in which dreams have died
- Ⓑ the poet's fears about life
- Ⓒ the glories of flying
- Ⓓ the poet's dream

THINK ABOUT THE ANSWER

Option A is the answer. The poem actually says that if dreams die, life is a broken-winged bird that cannot fly. Not all poems make their symbolism as clear as this one.

NOW YOU TRY IT

2 Identify a symbol in the second stanza. Explain what it symbolizes and why it is an appropriate symbol.

_____

_____

_____

Check your answer on page 109.

Circle It

If you scan the questions first and find you're going to be asked about symbolism, circle possible symbols as you read a poem or story. Then you can find them quickly when you need to refer to them in an answer.

KNOW THE SKILL: **MAKE INFERENCES**

An **inference** is similar to a conclusion or a generalization: you need to take what the author tells you and go beyond it to make a statement. When you make an inference, you "put two and two together" by analyzing the author's words and using your own thinking skills.

DURING THE TEST

As you read, look for events or ideas that must be true, based on what you read and what you know from experience. Use your knowledge of how things occur in life to "fill in the blanks" that an author doesn't fill in for you.

TEST EXAMPLE

1. What can you infer about Langston Hughes' attitude towards dreams?
   - Ⓐ   Winter is a depressing time of year.
   - Ⓑ   People who lose their dreams are foolish.
   - Ⓒ   Dreams are very important in living a full and happy life.
   - Ⓓ   One of the best ways to be happy is to keep birds as pets.

THINK ABOUT THE ANSWER

Option C is the answer. You know that the author considers dreams important to life because he compares the lack of dreams with a bird that cannot fly and a barren field. The other choices are not supported by the text.

NOW YOU TRY IT

2. Make an inference about how Langston Hughes learned about the effect on life of broken dreams.

   _____

   _____

   _____

   _____

Check your answer on page 109.

Practice Skimming

Skim through your reading materials before you read them so you can get in the practice of skimming. When you skim, you read the headers and pick up on the ideas presented.

Reading

KNOW THE SKILL: MAPS

You may be asked to read a map on some tests. You could be asked to give or follow directions, based on a map, or find specific places, directions, routes, or distances.

DURING THE TEST

Begin by reviewing the map so you're sure you know what it shows. Find the compass rose, key, scale, and other symbols, which tell you what different symbols on the map mean. Notice which other features are labeled.

TEST EXAMPLE

1 If you were driving from Las Cruces to the airport, what general direction would you be traveling?

Ⓐ east

Ⓑ south

Ⓒ southeast

Ⓓ northwest

Las Cruces

N
W ⊕ E
S

NM
TX

United States

El Paso Airport
El Paso

Mexico

Ciudad Juárez

Rio Graude

Scale in Miles

0   25   50

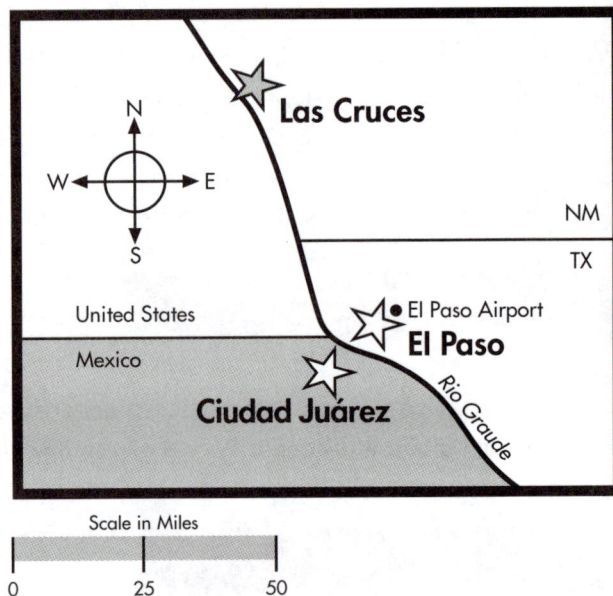

THINK ABOUT THE ANSWER

Option C is the answer. Option A leads away from Texas, as does option D. Option B leads to Mexico.

NOW YOU TRY IT

2 About how many miles would a round trip from Las Cruces to the airport in El Paso be?

Ⓕ 50 miles

Ⓖ 100 miles

Ⓗ 200 miles

Ⓙ 400 miles

Check your answer on page 109.

Advantage Test Prep Grade 7 © 2005 Creative Teaching Press

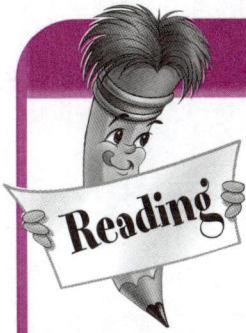

Reading

KNOW THE SKILL: **GRAPHS**

Graphs show numerical information quickly and clearly in picture form. There are many different kinds of graphs. Line graphs show the change in things over time. Bar graphs show comparisons between different pieces of information. Tests usually ask you to read and answer questions about different kinds of graphs.

DURING THE TEST

Read the graph title, along with labels, notes, legends, and any other information that is provided. Then use the information from the graph to eliminate incorrect answers and find the correct one.

TEST EXAMPLE

1 How many takeoffs are there between 7 and 8 AM?

    Ⓐ   9
    Ⓑ   12
    Ⓒ   19
    Ⓓ   26

Daily Takeoffs

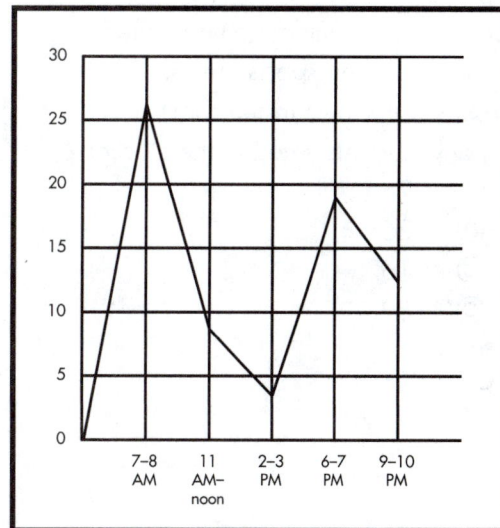

THINK ABOUT THE ANSWER

Option D is the correct answer. You find this by locating the point for the 7–8 AM time period and reading its value on the vertical scale. Option A is the number of takeoffs and landings for 11 AM–noon. Option B is the number of takeoffs and landings for 9–10 PM. Option C is the number of takeoffs and landings for 6–7 PM.

NOW YOU TRY IT

2 Write a general statement explaining the pattern of airport use, based on the information in the line graph.

_____

_____

Check your answer on page 109.

GRAPHIC INFORMATION

KNOW THE SKILL: CHARTS

Another useful way to show numerical information is the pie chart. Pie charts are especially good for showing how parts of the whole relate to each other and to the whole. They can be used to show what fraction or percentage each part of the whole represents.

DURING THE TEST

On a test, begin by reading the pie chart's title. Then examine the labels, notes, legend and any other information that is provided. Use the information from the chart to eliminate incorrect answers and find the correct one.

TEST EXAMPLE

1 Students at a new middle school voted on a name for their sports teams. The results are shown in the chart. How many students voted in the election?

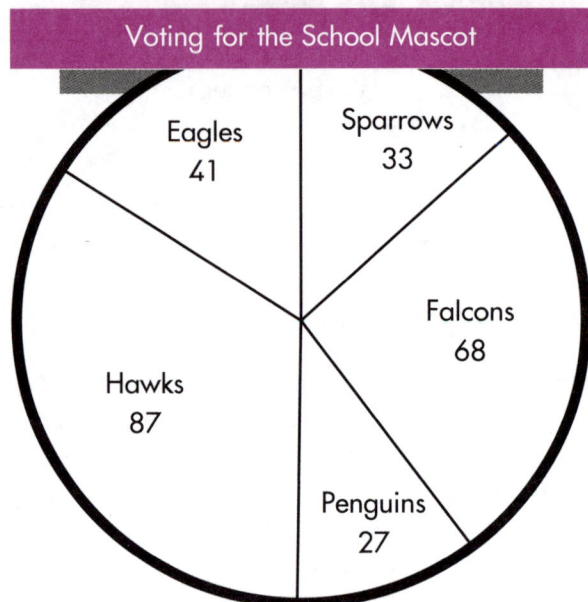

(A) 265
(B) 256
(C) 167
(D) 89

Voting for the School Mascot

Eagles 41
Sparrows 33
Falcons 68
Hawks 87
Penguins 27

THINK ABOUT THE ANSWER

Option B is the correct answer. To find it, add up all the votes for all the choices, for a total of 256 votes.

NOW YOU TRY IT

2 Which two choices when combined received exactly half the votes?

(F) Falcons and Eagles
(G) Eagles and Hawks
(H) Penguins and Hawks
(J) Penguins and Falcons

Check your answer on page 109.

Advantage Test Prep Grade 7 © 2005 Creative Teaching Press

Reading

KNOW THE SKILL: **TIME LINES**

A time line is a special kind of chart that helps you see dates of important events in order. Time lines are good for showing which events happened before or after others. A test may ask you to read and answer questions about a time line.

DURING THE TEST

Begin by scanning the time line, looking at the range. The range is the total length of time the time line covers. Most time lines are also marked off into lengths of time, like a ruler. The dates of the events are placed in relation to the marked lengths of time. The time line on this page is marked off into spans of 50 years for ease of reading.

TEST EXAMPLE

Time Line of Flight

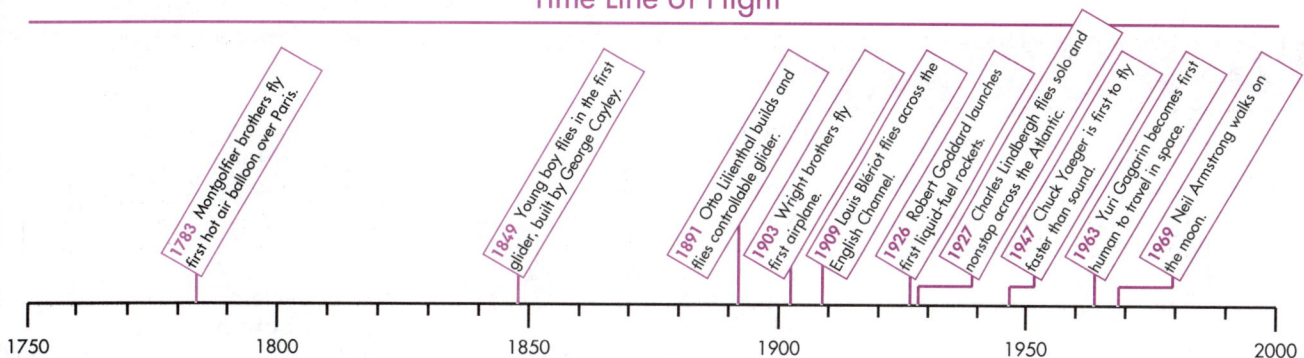

1783 Montgolfier brothers fly first hot air balloon over Paris.

1849 Young boy flies in the first glider, built by George Cayley.

1891 Otto Lilienthal builds and flies controllable glider.

1903 Wright brothers fly first airplane.

1909 Louis Blériot flies across the English Channel.

1926 Robert Goddard launches first liquid-fuel rockets.

1927 Charles Lindbergh flies solo and nonstop across the Atlantic.

1947 Chuck Yaeger is first to fly faster than sound.

1963 Yuri Gagarin becomes first human to travel in space.

1969 Neil Armstrong walks on the moon.

1750   1800   1850   1900   1950   2000

1 About how many years passed between the first and the last events shown on the time line?
- Ⓐ about 150
- Ⓒ about 250
- Ⓑ about 200
- Ⓓ about 275

THINK ABOUT THE ANSWER

Option B is the answer. 203 years passed between 1783, the date of the first event, and 1986, the date of the last event. Don't be misled that the time line itself begins with 1750 and ends with 2000.

NOW YOU TRY IT

2 Which two events occurred the closest together?
- Ⓕ Robert Goddard launches first liquid-fuel rockets; Charles Lindbergh flies solo and nonstop across the Atlantic.
- Ⓖ Yuri Gagarin becomes first human to travel in space; Neil Armstrong walks on the moon.
- Ⓗ Otto Lilienthal builds and flies controllable glider; Wright brothers fly first airplane.
- Ⓙ Louis Blériot flies across the English Channel; Wright brothers fly first airplane.

Check your answer on page 109.

Reading

KNOW THE SKILL: INDEX

An index is a list at the back of a book that tells you what subjects are covered in the book and on which pages. Looking at an index is a quick way to find out if the book covers the topic in which you're interested.

DURING THE TEST

Memorize these simple rules about indexes: a dash or hyphen between two page numbers means that all the pages between these two numbers contain information on the topic. When you see a series of pages separated by commas, there is information on the topic on each page, but not on the pages between them.

TEST EXAMPLE

INDEX

airfoil, 4–6
Armstrong, Neil, 82–83
Bernoulli effect, 4–6
birds, 6–7
Blériot, Louis, 51–53
Cayley, George, 33–35
Challenger, 86
Daedalus and
    Icarus, 11–12

da Vinci, Leonardo, 14,
    15
gravity, 9, 11
Gagarin, Yuri, 76
Glenn, John, 76, 77
hot–air balloons, 22–27
jets, 57–62
lift, 4–7
Lilienthal, Otto, 34–36
Lindbergh, Charles,
    51–55

moon landing, 79–81
NASA (National
    Aeronautics and Space
    Administration), 76, 79,
    86
rockets, 68, 76
solar system, 67–70
sound barrier, 63, 66,
    69
Wright brothers, 42–49
Yaeger, Chuck, 69

1 On what pages would you look in this book for a report on space exploration?

_____

_____

THINK ABOUT THE ANSWER

A possible answer is: The pages between 76 and 86 deal with space exploration, including the following topics: Armstrong, Neil; the Challenger; Gagarin, Yuri; Glenn, John; the moon landing; and rockets. Additional information might be found on pages 67–70 (solar system) and 9 and 11 (gravity).

NOW YOU TRY IT

2 Which is the most likely title for this book?

  Ⓕ   Exploring Space   Ⓗ   Early Pioneers of Flight

  Ⓖ   Hot-Air Balloons   Ⓙ   Into the Skies: The History of Flight

Check your answer on page 110.

KNOW THE SKILL: DICTIONARY ENTRY

A dictionary entry provides more than the correct spelling. It also tells you how to pronounce and define the word. It also offers the syllabication, part (or parts) of speech, and even synonyms, usage tips, and the history of the word. Knowing how to use a dictionary will help you on school assignments and as well as in everyday life.

DURING THE TEST

When answering a test question about dictionary entries, first skim the entry. Next, read the question, which will tell you what information you're looking for in the entry. Then go back to the entry and choose the correct answer.

TEST EXAMPLE

1 Read the dictionary entry and answer the questions.

tro·po·sphere (trõ′pə-sfir′,trõp′ə-) *n.* The lowest region of the earth's atmosphere, reaching about 17 km at the equator; the site of most weather phenomena. — **tro′·po·spher′·ic** (-sfer′ik, -sfer′-) *adj.*

Which word rhymes with the vowel in the first syllable of *troposphere*?

    Ⓐ thought   Ⓒ true
    Ⓑ throw   Ⓓ towel

THINK ABOUT THE ANSWER

Option B is correct. *Throw*, with a *long o*, rhymes with the first syllable of *troposphere*. The *o* with the short line above it means the *o* is pronounced like *oh*.

NOW YOU TRY IT

2 How is the word *troposphere* related to its Greek roots?

_____

_____

_____

Check your answer on page 110.

Keep Learning New Words

Continually expand your vocabulary. You can do this by reading books, magazines, and newspapers. You can use your fabulous vocabulary to score better on tests.

Introduction to Writing

Many tests will ask you to write several paragraphs about a topic to see how well you write. You may be asked to write fiction or nonfiction. You might describe your thoughts or feelings, or you may have to explain how to do something.

The test will usually give you a topic to write about, called a **writing prompt**. A writing prompt can be a statement or a question. Here are some examples of writing prompts:

- Read a story, and then write another story like it.
- Read a story, and then predict what happens next or write about the characters.
- Write a letter or postcard as if you are on a trip to some place you always wanted to go.
- Explain a step-by-step procedure, like making popcorn, or how to do something, like riding a bicycle.
- Write about a memory, such as your first cooking lesson or your first loose tooth.
- Write about a real or fictitious person you would like to invite to speak to your class.
- Write about something you like or don't like, such as being the oldest, youngest, or only child in your family.
- Look at a picture and then write about it. The picture might be a rainy day, people having a quarrel, children laughing, or something else.
- Explain your opinion on a topic and give reasons to support it.

Always read a writing prompt carefully so that you understand what you are supposed to do. Here are some general tips before you start writing:

- If you are asked to write a story, include characters with names.
- Give your story a beginning, a middle, and an end.
- Make sure the events in the story are in the correct order.
- Think through and plan every event carefully.
- If you are asked to explain how to do something, put the steps in chronological order. Make sure you explain each step thoroughly.
- If you are to write about a picture, tell about what any people in it might feel and think.
- If you are asked to write nonfiction, include many details to support your main ideas.
- Write a draft, read it, make any necessary changes, and rewrite it.
- Read your final draft carefully. Make sure that you followed all of the instructions in the writing prompt.
- Carefully check your spelling, punctuation, language usage, and grammar.
- Use good penmanship.

Advantage Test Prep Grade 7 © 2005 Creative Teaching Press

Writing

On most proficiency or standardized tests, someone will read your writing and use a rubric to score it. Many tests use a 4-point scoring rubric. The top score in each category is 4, while 0 is the lowest. Here is what a typical rubric looks like.

SCORING RUBRIC

Score	Content and Ideas	Organization	Sentence Structure and Clarity	Spelling, Punctuation, Usage, and Grammar
4	Excellent, well-developed ideas	Ideas are presented in a logical order	Sentences are complete and easy to understand	No more than two mistakes
3	Most ideas are well-developed	Most ideas are in a logical order	Most sentences are complete and easy to understand	No more than five mistakes
2	Some ideas do not relate to the topic or subject	Some ideas are in order	Some sentences are complete and easy to understand	No more than seven mistakes
1	Most ideas do not relate to the topic or subject	Few ideas are in order	Few sentences are complete and easy to understand	No more than ten mistakes
0	Little or no work completed	Little or no work completed	Little or no work completed	Little or no work completed

The person scoring your writing will give you a score for each category and then add the scores. In a rubric like this one, the highest score is 16.

To score well on the writing section of a test, you must make sure your writing exactly follows what the writing prompt asks you to do. Your ideas have to be carefully thought through. You must organize them in a way that makes sense and is easy for the reader to follow. You must write in complete, error-free sentences.

BRAINSTORMING AND ORGANIZING YOUR IDEAS

Writing

When you are writing for a test, your time will be limited. You'll have to think clearly and quickly to organize your ideas. Graphic organizers, such as those below, can help you get started.

MAIN IDEA CHART

Your main ideas should be supported with details. This chart will help you organize your ideas and make sure you have details to back them up. You could make a chart for each main idea.

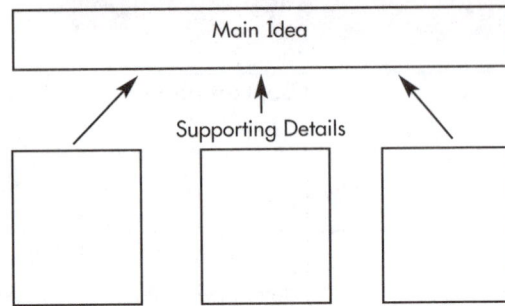

Main Idea

Supporting Details

SEQUENCE CHART

A sequence chart is a good way to organize the steps in a procedure or the events in a story. Complete the chart and then write paragraphs about the topics in the order on the chart.

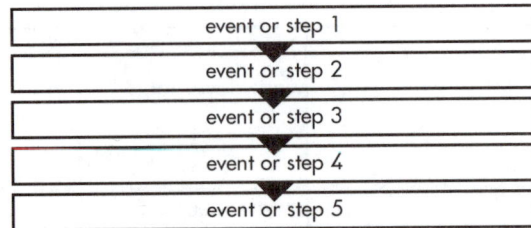

event or step 1
event or step 2
event or step 3
event or step 4
event or step 5

STORY PLANNER

A story planner helps you to brainstorm the problem your characters will solve and how they will try to solve it.

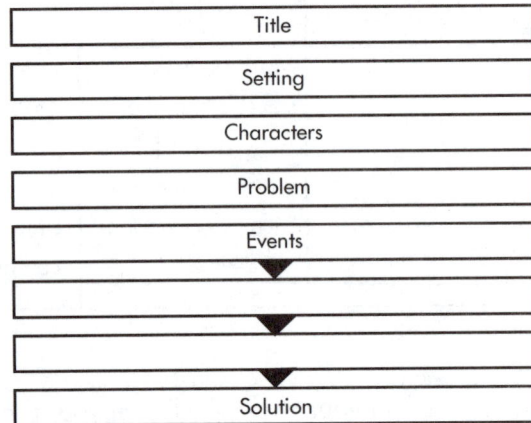

Title

Setting

Characters

Problem

Events

Solution

VENN DIAGRAM

If a writing prompt asks you to compare or contrast two or more things, a Venn diagram is a good way to organize likenesses (in the overlapping part) and differences (in the parts that do not overlap).

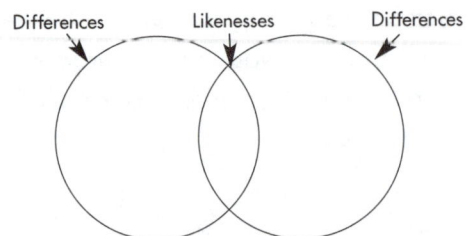

Differences   Likenesses   Differences

Advantage Test Prep Grade 7 © 2005 Creative Teaching Press

You have decided to have a surprise birthday party for a friend. Planning a surprise party is a big job. Decide what things you'll have to do—and the order in which you'll have to do them. Then write a detailed plan describing each step you will take to organize the party. Be sure to include details like dates, number of guests, activities, and supplies. Use this graphic organizer to help you get started planning and writing your first draft

Writing

Write your first draft on this page and the next.
Use separate sheets of paper if you need more room.

_____

_____

_____

_____

_____

_____

_____

_____

_____

_____

_____

_____

_____

_____

EDIT YOUR FIRST DRAFT

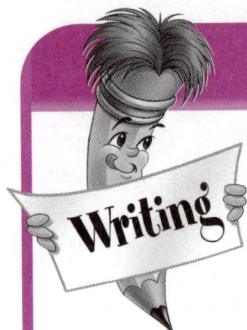

Between your first draft and your final writing comes a very important step. It's when you take a good look at your writing and find ways to make it better. The step is called editing. It's not the same as writing, because you're not changing everything—just making what you have written better.

USING A CHECK LIST

Responding to a prompt like this one, maybe you notice that you haven't fully explained an important step or that you've included too much unnecessary information. This writer's checklist can help you analyze your first draft and spot places you need to improve.

WRITER'S CHECKLIST

You will earn your best score if:

☐ your paragraphs are written in a logical order.

☐ readers can easily understand your plans for the party.

☐ you have included every necessary step and piece of information.

☐ you have not included unimportant things that the reader does not need to know.

☐ you have not repeated information unnecessarily.

☐ the details you make up are realistic and appropriate.

☐ you make no spelling, grammar, punctuation, or capitalization errors.

Advantage Test Prep Grade 7 © 2005 Creative Teaching Press

WRITE YOUR FINAL DRAFT

Before you start your final draft, use the checklist on page 36 to review your first draft. Make sure you've covered the important points in the checklist, and look for other ways to improve the content, organization, clarity, and grammar of your first draft. Then write your final draft.

_____

_____

_____

_____

_____

_____

_____

_____

_____

_____

_____

_____

_____

_____

_____

WRITE YOUR FINAL DRAFT

_____

_____

_____

_____

_____

_____

_____

_____

_____

_____

_____

_____

_____

_____

_____

_____

_____

_____

_____

_____

_____

_____

_____

_____

Go back to the writing rubric on page 31. Use the rubric to score your work. Give yourself a score from 4 to 0 for each category. Then ask someone else to score your writing. Compare and talk about the scores.

How I Scored It

Content and Ideas	Organization	Sentence Structure and Clarity	Spelling, Punctuation, Usage, and Grammar
_____	_____	_____	_____

How Someone Else Scored It

Content and Ideas	Organization	Sentence Structure and Clarity	Spelling, Punctuation, Usage, and Grammar
_____	_____	_____	_____

Few skills you can learn will be as valuable as your language skills. Think about how often—in school, at home, and with your friends—you need to communicate clearly with other people.

There are many different language skills that help us use English well. Some of the skills you can expect to see on a test are spelling, grammar, punctuation, sentence formation, and paragraph organization. Mastering these skills will help you do better on tests. These skills also form the foundation for success in many other challenges you will meet in school and later on in life.

One of the best ways to improve your language skills is to read. Whenever you read, you learn how language is used. The more you read, the more it becomes part of you.

Here is a list of key skills you will learn and practice in this section:

- Punctuation and Capitalization
- Hyphens
- Parentheses and Brackets
- Commas and Semicolons
- Infinitives and Participles
- Gerunds and Gerund Phrases
- Pronouns and Antecedents
- Parts of Speech
- Types of Sentences
- Compound Sentences
- Negative Sentences
- Paragraph Construction
- Spelling

Advantage Test Prep Grade 7 © 2005 Creative Teaching Press

Language

KNOW THE SKILL: **PUNCTUATION AND CAPITALIZATION**

Every sentence must end with an end mark. Use a period to end a sentence that is a statement or command. Use a question mark for questions. Use an exclamation point for sentences that express strong emotion. Proper nouns and adjectives, along with the first word in a sentence, must begin with a capital letter. Proper nouns are the names of specific people, places, events, organizations, and other things. Proper adjectives are based on proper nouns.

DURING THE TEST

Check to see if a noun or adjective refers to something or someone specific. If it does, it should begin with a capital letter. While reading each sentence, decide whether it is a statement, command, exclamation, or question. Then you'll know which end mark it needs.

TEST EXAMPLE

1 Choose the sentence that uses correct punctuation and capitalization.
- Ⓐ do you think the Spacecraft will reach Jupiter safely?
- Ⓑ Do you think the spacecraft will reach jupiter safely.
- Ⓒ Do you think the spacecraft will reach Jupiter safely?
- Ⓓ Do you think the spacecraft will reach jupiter safely!

THINK ABOUT THE ANSWER

The answer is C. *Do*, the first word of the sentence, is capitalized, as well as *Jupiter*, a proper noun. The sentence ends with a question mark. In option A, *do* should be capitalized, and *Spacecraft* should not be capitalized because it is not a proper noun. In option B, *jupiter* should be capitalized. Because the sentence is a question, it should end with a question mark. In option D, *jupiter* should be capitalized. The sentence does not express strong emotion, so it should not end with an exclamation point.

NOW YOU TRY IT

2 Choose the sentence that uses correct punctuation and capitalization.
- Ⓕ Dad asked if we wanted to see the egyptian mummy at the History Museum.
- Ⓖ Dad asked if we wanted to see the Egyptian mummy at the history museum.
- Ⓗ dad asked if we wanted to see the Egyptian Mummy at the history museum.
- Ⓙ Dad asked if we wanted to see the egyptian mummy at the history museum?

Check your answer on page 110.

Get Testwise

Use the Process of Elimination
On multiple choice questions, first rule out answers that you know are wrong. Then rule out answers that are partly wrong or don't seem to fit. If two options are very similar they might both be incorrect. This process will help narrow down possible answers.

Language

KNOW THE SKILL: HYPHENS

Use a hyphen to join words, that when put together, make up a single adjective such as *well-to-do* and *good-looking*. Another use of the hyphen is in spelled-out compound numbers from twenty-one to ninety-nine. A third use of hyphens is in fractions when they are used as modifiers: *The play I'm writing is one-half finished.* Do not use a hyphen when a fraction is used as a noun: *Three fourths of the students live in apartments.*

DURING THE TEST

As you read, keep in mind the ways hyphens are used—and don't confuse a hyphen (-) with a dash (—), which is longer and has different uses.

TEST EXAMPLE

1 Choose the sentence that uses hyphenation correctly.
- Ⓐ The director gave certificates to two-thirds of the volunteers.
- Ⓑ Mr. Li's car is the best looking one in the whole parade.
- Ⓒ Monica is the most self-centered person I've ever met.
- Ⓓ Fifty five people entered the spelling contest.

THINK ABOUT THE ANSWER

Option C is correct. *Self-centered* is a single adjective. In option A, *two thirds* is used as a noun. Therefore, it should not have a hyphen. In option B, a hyphen is needed in the adjective *best-looking*. In option D, a hyphen is needed in the number *fifty-five*.

NOW YOU TRY IT

2 Choose the sentence that uses hyphenation correctly.
- Ⓕ The recycling drive is three fourths finished, but a lot of work is left.
- Ⓖ Next to the garbage can was a very mean-sounding dog.
- Ⓗ The winner received seventy five dollars and a book.
- Ⓙ The hard to see rowboat was rammed by the ferry.

Check your answer on page 110.

Get Testwise

Use a Dictionary
Knowing which words to hyphenate and which not to can be tricky. The best guide is a dictionary. When in doubt, look up the word. Then you'll know how it should be treated when you see it on a test.

Advantage Test Prep Grade 7 © 2005 Creative Teaching Press

Language

KNOW THE SKILL: PARENTHESES AND BRACKETS

Parentheses enclose material that is apart from the main thought of a sentence. For example, *If you come to the party (and I really hope you do), bring your CDs.* Include the correct end mark if the material in parentheses is a question or exclamation. Brackets are used to insert extra material in a quotation from another writer: *"Captain Rogers signed the paper [explaining his actions during the battle] and placed it in a leather pouch."*

DURING THE TEST

On a test, brackets will usually only appear in a sentence that also uses quotation marks.

TEST EXAMPLE

1 Which sentence is correct?

 Ⓐ The new Russell Crowe movie [did you like Gladiator?] is coming to the mall.
 Ⓑ What was Nicholas thinking (when he crossed the street without looking?)
 Ⓒ Are you thinking of asking Devin (he's really nice!) to the picnic?
 Ⓓ The last question the one about the Aztecs was really tough.

THINK ABOUT THE ANSWER

Option C is correct. The words *he's really nice*! are apart from the main thought of the sentence. Option A should use parentheses, not brackets. In option B, *when he crossed the street without looking* should not be in parentheses. It is an important part of the sentence, not apart from its meaning. In option D, *the one about the Aztecs* should be in parentheses because it is apart from the main meaning of the sentence.

NOW YOU TRY IT

2 Which sentence is correct?

 Ⓕ "Four score and seven [eighty-seven] years ago," Lincoln wrote in the Gettysburg Address.
 Ⓖ Place the red cylinder [do not confuse it with the brown tube] on the spindle.
 Ⓗ (Have you decided which shirt) I like the blue one best to buy?
 Ⓙ Kara lives in the house (next to the park).

Check your answer on page 110.

Get Testwise

Don't Be Absurd!
Absurd choices are usually wrong. You can quickly rule them out.

KNOW THE SKILL: COMMAS AND SEMICOLONS

An independent clause has both a subject and a verb and can stand alone as a sentence. When a sentence joins two independent clauses, separate them with a comma and a conjunction such as *and, but, or, so,* or *yet*. Two independent clauses can also be joined by a semicolon. A dependent clause lacks a subject or a verb. Use a comma to set off a dependent clause when it begins a sentence. Also use a comma to set off an interruption in a sentence.

Correct: *I feed the cat, but my brother cleans the litter box.*
Correct: *I feed the cat; my brother cleans the litter box.*
Correct: *Rubbing against my leg, the cat purred loudly.*
Correct: *All right, Miss Puss, I'll feed you!*

DURING THE TEST

Look for both verbs and subjects in independent clauses. It they are there, you need to use a comma and conjunction or a semicolon to join them.

TEST EXAMPLE

1 Which sentence is correct?
   Ⓐ   Watch out, Michael that hay bale is tipping.
   Ⓑ   You can lead a horse to water yet you can't make it drink.
   Ⓒ   With a wave of his wand; the magician made the rabbit disappear.
   Ⓓ   Mom and I changed the oil on the tractor; we couldn't fix the wheel rim.

THINK ABOUT THE ANSWER

The correct answer is option D. The two independent clauses are joined with a semicolon. In option A, there should be a comma following *Michael*, to set it off completely from the rest of the sentence.
In option B, a comma is required before *yet* because it joins two independent clauses in one sentence.
In option C, a comma should follow *wand* because it is the last word of a dependent clause.

NOW YOU TRY IT

2 Which sentence is correct?
   Ⓕ   That car is awesome, do you know what kind it is?
   Ⓖ   The librarian Mr. Thomas knows a lot about authors.
   Ⓗ   After the clock struck one, all the people at the dance went home.
   Ⓙ   The night was cold and rainy; and it started snowing in the morning.

Check your answer on page 110.

Language

KNOW THE SKILL: INFINITIVES AND PARTICIPLES

An **infinitive** is a form of a verb that usually begins with the word *to*. It usually is used as a noun. For example, *Maria really loves to read.* The infinitive is used as the direct object of the sentence and answers the question *What does Maria love?*

A **participle** is another form of the verb that can be used as an adjective to modify a noun. A present participle ends in *-ing*. A past participle usually ends in *-ed*.

Present participle: *Sitting at the curb, we watched the parade.*
Past participle: *The picture painted by Matisse is hanging in the gallery.*

DURING THE TEST

Although the word *to* signals an infinitive, it is also used as a preposition: *Did you send that e-mail to Becca?* Check to see how *to* is used in the sentences you come across on a test. Not all words that end in *-ed* are past participles. Many are simply the past tense of a verb: *Matthew tuned his guitar.* In the same way, many words that end in *-ing* are not present participles. They are the present progressive tense of a verb: *I am eating an apple.* Used this way, the *-ing* word will be preceded by *am, are, is,* was, or *were.*

TEST EXAMPLE

1 Which sentence correctly uses an infinitive?
- Ⓐ A document created in HTML can be sent over the Internet.
- Ⓑ The woman swimming in the pool won an Olympic medal.
- Ⓒ To knit is my grandmother's very favorite hobby.
- Ⓓ Robert's family went to Virginia Beach in July.

THINK ABOUT THE ANSWER

Option C is correct. The infinitive is *To knit* and is used as the subject. The *to* in option D is used as a preposition, with *Virginia Beach* as its object. In option A, *created* is a past participle. In option B, *swimming* is a present participle.

NOW YOU TRY IT

2 Which sentence correctly uses a past participle?
- Ⓕ Baked by the sun, the grocery store parking lot was very hot.
- Ⓖ Feeling he was wrong, the man admitted his mistake.
- Ⓗ Mr. DiAntonio baked the pizzas in a large oven.
- Ⓙ Are you sure you're feeling OK?

Check your answer on page 110.

Language

KNOW THE SKILL: GERUNDS AND GERUND PHRASES

A **gerund** is a form of the verb ending in *-ing* that is used like a noun. It can be used as a subject or object.

> Gerund used as a subject: *Jogging is a good form of exercise.*
>
> Gerund used as a direct object: *Other people prefer swimming.*

Gerunds usually occur in gerund phrases. Gerund phrases include a gerund and other words that modify it.

> Gerund phrase used as a subject: <u>*Jogging on a path*</u> *is a good form of exercise.*
>
> Gerund phrase used as a direct object: *Other people prefer* <u>*swimming in a pool*</u>.

DURING THE TEST

As you learned in the last lesson, some words ending in *-ing* are not gerunds. They can be present participles or present progressive verb tenses. Knowing how the *-ing* word is used will help you identify it.

TEST EXAMPLE

1 Which sentence correctly uses a gerund?

- Ⓐ   Feeling sick, I couldn't eat a thing.
- Ⓑ   What's that blue stuff Jeremy is eating?
- Ⓒ   The team members are feeling very proud of their victory.
- Ⓓ   With my stomach upset, eating is the last thing on my mind.

THINK ABOUT THE ANSWER

The correct answer is option D. The word *eating* is a gerund used as the subject of the sentence. In option A, *Feeling* is a present participle. In option B, *is eating* is the verb. In option C, *are feeling* is the verb.

NOW YOU TRY IT

2 Which sentence correctly uses a gerund phrase?

- Ⓕ   Grandpa enjoys telling people about his trips.
- Ⓖ   Traveling gives you lots of great experiences.
- Ⓗ   Grandpa is planning a trip now to South America.
- Ⓙ   Listening to him, I'd like to go with him on a trip one day.

Check your answer on page 110.

Get Testwise

Know What You're Answering

Read the question very carefully. Look for key words, such as the word *phrase* in the question above, that will tell you exactly what answer the test is looking for.

KNOW THE SKILL: PRONOUNS AND ANTECEDENTS

Pronouns are words that take the place of nouns, or that refer to nouns in a sentence. When a pronoun refers to a word in a sentence, that word is called the **antecedent**. An antecedent must agree with its pronoun in number (singular or plural) and gender (feminine, masculine, or neuter).

DURING THE TEST

Make sure you can identify the pronoun or antecedent in a sentence. If you are asked to provide a pronoun, knowing the antecedent will allow you to choose a pronoun that agrees in number and gender. If you are asked to provide an antecedent, knowing the pronoun will allow you to choose an antecedent that agrees in number and gender.

TEST EXAMPLE

1 Choose the answer that best completes the sentence.

Bethany's math book has lost _____ cover.
- Ⓐ her
- Ⓑ his
- Ⓒ its
- Ⓓ their

THINK ABOUT THE ANSWER

Option C is correct. The pronoun *its* agrees in number (singular) and gender (neuter) with *book*. In option A, the singular feminine pronoun *her* does not agree in gender with the singular neuter noun *book*. In option B, *his* (masculine, singular) does not agree in gender with *book*. In option D, the plural pronoun *their* does not agree in number with *book*.

NOW YOU TRY IT

2 Choose the answer that best completes the sentence.

When _____ got home from school, they found that the door was locked.
- Ⓕ David and Sam
- Ⓗ Sam
- Ⓖ my mom
- Ⓙ she

Check your answer on page 110.

Get Testwise

I Know This!
Knowing how a pronoun is used is the key to getting a question correct on a test. Review the different ways they are used as you prepare for a test.

KNOW THE SKILL: PARTS OF SPEECH

There are eight kinds of words. They are called **parts of speech**. They include nouns, which name persons, places, things, or ideas; pronouns, which replace or refer to nouns; verbs, which show actions; adjectives, which describe nouns; adverbs, which describe verbs; prepositions, which show relationships; conjunctions, which join parts of sentences; and interjections, which express strong feeling. You may be asked to identify any of these parts of speech.

DURING THE TEST

Word endings can be clues to identifying parts of speech. Adjectives often end in *-ish*, *-y*, or *-ful*. Many adverbs end in *-ly*. Be careful, though. Verbs can end in *-s*, but so can plural nouns.

TEST EXAMPLE

1   Which sentence contains an adverb?
- Ⓐ   The cat walked into the room.
- Ⓑ   The quiet cat walked into the room.
- Ⓒ   The cat walked into the quiet room.
- Ⓓ   The cat walked quietly into the room.

THINK ABOUT THE ANSWER

Option D is correct. *Quietly* is an adverb; its describes how the cat walked. Option A does not contain an adverb or an adjective. In option B, *quiet* is an adjective that describes the cat. In option C, the adjective *quiet* describes the room.

NOW YOU TRY IT

2   Which sentence does NOT contain a preposition?
- Ⓕ   Melanie hit the ball toward the shortstop.
- Ⓖ   There's nothing good on TV tonight.
- Ⓗ   Does your father like to play tennis?
- Ⓙ   Did you look under the couch?

Check your answer on page 110.

Get Testwise

Have a Positive Attitude
A positive attitude helps in all you do. Have self-confidence and think positive.

KNOW THE SKILL: TYPES OF SENTENCES

The four types of sentences are declarative, interrogative, imperative, and exclamatory. A **declarative sentence** makes a statement or expresses a fact. It ends with a period. An **interrogative sentence** asks a question and ends with a question mark. An **imperative sentence** expresses a command or request. It often ends with a period. If it expresses strong emotion, it can end with an exclamation point. An **exclamatory sentence** expresses surprise or strong emotion and ends with an exclamation point.

DURING THE TEST

Look for hints in the sentences themselves that can help you identify them. Imperative sentences usually omit the subject, which is often you. Exclamatory sentences often omit the verb. Interrogative sentences often place part of the verb before the subject. Declarative sentences, however, usually follow subject-verb-object order.

TEST EXAMPLE

1 Which of the following is an imperative sentence?
- Ⓐ What a beautiful ring!
- Ⓑ Don't touch the wet paint.
- Ⓒ Have you ever been to a soccer game?
- Ⓓ A family of squirrels lives in the tree outside my window.

THINK ABOUT THE ANSWER

The correct answer is option B. It gives a command. Option A is an exclamatory sentence. Option C is an interrogative sentence. Option D is a declarative sentence.

NOW YOU TRY IT

2 Which of the following is NOT a declarative sentence?
- Ⓕ I picked some flowers this morning.
- Ⓖ There's a huge lilac bush in the yard.
- Ⓗ My mother says the bush might be a hundred years old.
- Ⓙ Please put the flowers in the vase on the dining room table.

Check your answer on page 110.

Watch for Certain Words

Keep an eye out for words such as *not, but,* and *except*. These words place limits on the answer. Also watch out for absolute words such as *always, never,* and *only*. If one of these words is in a question, it means there can be no exceptions.

Language

KNOW THE SKILL: COMPOUND SENTENCES

A simple sentence is made up of one independent clause: *The geese swim on the pond.* The compound sentence is two or more simple sentences joined by a conjunction (*and, or, but, yet, so*) and a comma, or by a semicolon: *The geese swim on the pond, but the ducks sit on the shore.*

DURING THE TEST

Look for conjunctions or semicolons to help identify compound sentences. Watch out, however; conjunctions can also link compound subjects and compound verbs in simple sentences.

TEST EXAMPLE

1 Which of the following is a compound sentence?
- Ⓐ My aunt and uncle live in Colorado.
- Ⓑ They camp and hike in the Rocky Mountains.
- Ⓒ Aunt Jane is a lawyer, but Uncle Jack works for the state.
- Ⓓ My cousins are coming to visit us in Virginia next summer.

THINK ABOUT THE ANSWER

Option C is correct. The two independent clauses are *Aunt Jane is a lawyer* and *Uncle Jack works for the state*. They are joined by the conjunction *but*. The other choices are simple sentences. Option A has a compound subject. Option B has a compound verb. Option D has a simple subject and verb.

NOW YOU TRY IT

2 Which of the following is NOT a compound sentence?
- Ⓕ Lewis and Clark explored the western United States in the early 1800s.
- Ⓖ President Thomas Jefferson sent them, and they reported back to him.
- Ⓗ Lewis was Jefferson's assistant, but Clark was an army officer.
- Ⓙ The explorers faced many dangers, yet they returned safely.

Check your answer on page 110.

Get Testwise

Don't Prepare at the Last Minute

Give yourself time to relax before the test. Studying up to the last minute will cause you to be tense. Trying to learn new things right before the test might cause you to be confused about things you already know. Having a healthy relaxed attitude will help you handle the task coolly and confidently.

   Advantage Test Prep Grade 7 © 2005 Creative Teaching Press

KNOW THE SKILL: NEGATIVE SENTENCES

Negative sentences express the ideas of *not*, *no*, *none*, *nothing*, and *never*. Negative sentences often use *not* in contractions such as, *don't*, *didn't*, *aren't*, *isn't*, *can't*, *couldn't*, *haven't*, and *hasn't*. They also use words like *no*, *no one*, *nobody*, *none*, and *neither*. A sentence should use only one negative word to show that it is negative. An incorrect sentence with more than one negative word is called a **double negative**.

DURING THE TEST

Make sure you can identify the words used to make a sentence negative. If there are more than one in the sentence, it's wrong.

TEST EXAMPLE

1 Which sentence is correct?

- Ⓐ She didn't see none of the movies.
- Ⓑ We couldn't tell her nothing about them.
- Ⓒ Nobody can't find out when the film starts.
- Ⓓ No one was in the lobby after the long movie let out.

THINK ABOUT THE ANSWER

Option D is correct. It contains only a single negative, *no one*. All the others contain double negatives. In option A, *didn't* and *none* are negatives. In option B, *couldn't* and *nothing* are negatives. In option C, *nobody* and *can't* are negatives.

NOW YOU TRY IT

2 Which sentence is correct?

- Ⓕ Isn't there nothing good on TV?
- Ⓖ I'm not very fond of game shows.
- Ⓗ You haven't seen nothing better than this program!
- Ⓙ I didn't get no chance to watch it last time it was on.

Check your answer on page 110.

Have a Plan

Have a plan for answering every type of question. Some people like to answer easy questions within a section first because it might help with answering the harder questions later.

KNOW THE SKILL: PARAGRAPH CONSTRUCTION

A paragraph is made up of several parts. The **topic sentence** states the main idea of the paragraph. It is often the first sentence in the paragraph. Other sentences provide details that support the main idea of the topic sentence. Paragraphs also often have a closing sentence. It can restate the topic sentence, announce a conclusion, give the writer's personal opinion, or ask a question.

DURING THE TEST

Read the paragraph carefully. Try asking yourself, "If I were writing this paragraph, what would I use as a topic sentence or closing sentence?"

TEST EXAMPLE

1 Read the paragraph. Which sentence would make the best topic sentence?

Their webbed feet make swimming easy. They can travel up to a quarter of a mile under water without surfacing to breathe. Their slender bodies and flattened heads glide swiftly through rivers and streams. The otter's fur, highly prized by people, keeps it warm in cold water.

- Ⓐ   River otters live in rivers and streams of North America.
- Ⓑ   River otters are perfectly adapted to their environment.
- Ⓒ   River otters are one of the most interesting mammals.
- Ⓓ   River otters are related to weasels.

THINK ABOUT THE ANSWER

The correct answer is option B because the details in the paragraph discuss how well an otter's characteristics match its river environment. Options A and D are details that support the main idea. Option C is the writer's opinion.

NOW YOU TRY IT

2 Read the paragraph. Which sentence would make the best closing sentence?

Stock car racing, also known as *NASCAR*, was born in the southern United States in the late 1940s. Its popularity with racing fans has increased enormously over the years. Spectators love the thrilling action and blazing speed. NASCAR races often become all-day celebrations. Daredevil drivers like Richard Petty, Dale Earnhart, and Jeff Gordon have become well-known sports heroes.

- Ⓕ   One famous race is the Daytona 500.
- Ⓖ   Stock cars use special tires and modified engines.
- Ⓗ   Most observers expect NASCAR's popularity to continue to grow.
- Ⓙ   *NASCAR* stands for "National Association for Stock Car Auto Racing."

Check your answer on page 110.

KNOW THE SKILL: **INFLECTED ENDINGS**

Many words are spelled differently when endings are added. Some common endings, or inflections, that can cause spelling trouble, are -*able*, -*ly*, -*ness*, -*y*, and -*ed*. Learn the rules for these inflections. For example, for words that end in -*n*, keep the *n* when adding the ending –*ness*. Many words that end in *l* need another *l* before the ending –*ly*. For many words that end in *y*, the *y* is changed to an *i* when adding -*ed*.

DURING THE TEST

Try to think of a word that is spelled in a similar way to the one on the test. The test word might add an inflection in the same way. For example, *typically* is *typical* plus -*ly*, just like *finally* is *final* plus -*ly*.

TEST EXAMPLE

1 Choose the word that is spelled correctly to complete the sentence.

Raymond's _____ sometimes drives me crazy!

- Ⓐ stubbornness
- Ⓑ stubornness
- Ⓒ stubborness
- Ⓓ stubornness

THINK ABOUT THE ANSWER

Option A is correct. Following the rule, *stubborn* becomes *stubbornness* when the suffix -*ness* is added.

NOW YOU TRY IT

2 Choose the word that is spelled correctly to complete the sentence.

How many bags of garbage have you _____ to the trash bin?

- Ⓕ caried
- Ⓖ carried
- Ⓗ carryed
- Ⓙ carreyed

Check your answer on page 110.

Get Testwise

Trust Your Instincts

If you have a hunch about an answer, it is more likely to be the correct answer. Don't second guess your decisions and change your answers unless you have a very good reason to believe you made a mistake.

KNOW THE SKILL: FREQUENTLY MISSPELLED WORDS

Tests will ask you to identify misspelled words. There's no shortcut to being a good speller. The two keys are reading a lot and practicing.

DURING THE TEST

Many people misspell words with the letter combinations *ie* and *ei*. Remember this rule:

- *i* before *e*, except after *c*, or when sounded like *a*, as in *neighbor* or *weigh*.

TEST EXAMPLE

1 Look at the underlined words. Which is spelled incorrectly?

- Ⓐ The reindeer pulled a large <u>sliegh</u>.
- Ⓑ Duncan's older brother is very <u>conceited</u>.
- Ⓒ How did you do on last year's <u>achievement</u> tests?
- Ⓓ Most trains in this state carry <u>freight</u> rather than passengers.

THINK ABOUT THE ANSWER

The correct answer is option A. Because the sound is *long a*, as in *neighbor* and *weigh*, the correct spelling is *sleigh*. Option B is spelled *ei* because these letters follow *c*.

NOW YOU TRY IT

2 Look at the underlined words. Which is spelled correctly?

- Ⓕ The game was delayed <u>breifly</u> when a dog ran on the field.
- Ⓖ The bride wore a lovely <u>veil</u> made of white lace.
- Ⓗ It was quite a <u>releif</u> when the test was over.
- Ⓙ Would you like a <u>peice</u> of cheesecake?

Check your answer on page 110.

Read, Read, Read!

The best way to learn to spell is to read lots of different things. Books, magazines, and newspapers will let you see lots of words that are spelled correctly. The more you see, the better speller you'll become!

You will use your mathematics skills in school, at work, and in everyday life. Understanding mathematics will also help you to solve problems, think logically, and apply abstract reasoning. Most standardized tests feature a math section that asks you to apply a variety of skills. This section will help you sharpen your math skills and get you ready to do well on tests.

Here is a list of key skills you will learn and practice in this section:

- Comparing and Ordering Integers
- Converting Whole Numbers and Decimals to Scientific Notation
- Exponents
- Adding and Subtracting Fractions with Unlike Denominators
- Multiplying Integers
- Dividing Decimals
- Estimating to Predict Results
- Greatest Common Factor
- Prime Factorization
- Area of an Irregular Two-Dimensional Figure
- Volume of a Solid
- Surface Area of a Three-Dimensional Figure
- Pythagorean Relationship
- Congruence and Similarity
- Examining Shapes on a Coordinate Grid
- Evaluating Expressions
- Solving Equations with One Variable
- Graphing Linear Equations
- Finding Measures of Center and Spread
- Computing Probabilities for Simple and Compound Events
- Representing Data Graphically
- Solving a Multi-Step Problem
- Solving a Proportion Problem

Math

KNOW THE SKILL: **COMPARING AND ORDERING INTEGERS**

Compare and place numbers in order by comparing digits from left (larger) to right (smaller) until they are different. Use the symbols = (equals), < (less than), and > (greater than) in expressions.

DURING THE TEST

A way to remember what the "greater than" and "less than" symbols mean is that the "point" of the angle always points toward the smaller number. In the expression $8 < 10$, the point is toward the 8. In $7 > 2$, the point of the angle is toward 2.

TEST EXAMPLE

1 Which group of numbers is written in order from greatest to least?

- Ⓐ 6,320,998; 6,340,090; 6,337,508
- Ⓑ 4,197; 4,179; 4,791
- Ⓒ 66,104; 66,041; 66,014
- Ⓓ 334,004; 334,040; 334,400

THINK ABOUT THE ANSWER

The answer is option C. Comparing digits from left to right, you find that the 1 in 66,104 is greater than the 0 in 66,041. Therefore, the first number is greater than the second number. Comparing the second number to the third, you find that the 4 in 66,041 is greater than the 1 in 66,014. Therefore, the second number is greater than the third, and the three numbers are in order from greatest to least.

NOW YOU TRY IT

2 Which number correctly completes the expression?

$5,762,410 <$ _____

- Ⓕ 5,762,450
- Ⓖ 5,762,399
- Ⓗ 5,672,998
- Ⓙ 5,762,401

Check your answer on page 111.

Get Testwise

Don't Panic!

If you find that you are getting anxious before or during the test, take several slow, deep breaths to relax. Visualize being in a peaceful and calm place. Remind yourself that you are well prepared. Don't talk to other students before the test. Anxiety can be very contagious!

KNOW THE SKILL: CONVERTING WHOLE NUMBERS AND DECIMALS TO SCIENTIFIC NOTATION

Very large numbers are sometimes written in scientific notation. Scientific notation uses exponents of 10, multiplied by a smaller number, called the **base**, to represent large numbers. For example, light travels at a speed of about 18,000,000,000 (18 billion) meters per minute. Using scientific notation, this number can be written 1.8×10^{10} meters per minute. This notation means you multiply 1.8 by 10 ten times.

DURING THE TEST

An easy way to remember how many zeros to add to a number represented in scientific notation is to move the decimal point to the right the same number of places as the exponent.

TEST EXAMPLE

1 $2.5 \times 10^8 =$

- Ⓐ   2,500,000
- Ⓑ   25,000,000
- Ⓒ   250,000,000
- Ⓓ   2,500,000,000

THINK ABOUT THE ANSWER

The answer is option C. 2.5×10^8 means you multiply 2.5 times 10 eight times. Doing this gives you an answer of 250,000,000 (250 million). Notice the answer has eight places following the 2, and that the decimal point is gone. Don't forget to add commas, starting from the right.

NOW YOU TRY IT

2 $3.4 \times 10^6 =$ _____

- Ⓕ   340,000
- Ⓖ   3,400,000
- Ⓗ   34,000,000
- Ⓙ   340,000,000

Check your answer on page 111.

Get Testwise

It Can't Hurt!
You may want to count the zeroes represented by scientific notation twice—just to make sure you've got the right number.

KNOW THE SKILL: **EXPONENTS**

Working with exponents involves squares and square roots. A square is a number, called the base, multiplied by itself. A square is written 4^2 and means the same as 4×4. Both equal 16. The square root of a number is the factor which when multiplied by itself, equals the number. For example, the square root of 16 is 4: 4×4 equals 16.

DURING THE TEST

A test may ask you to write a number in exponential form or to translate a number written in exponential form into regular notation. You may also be asked to find the square root of a number. Using scrap paper will help you make notes about which places the various numbers should be in.

TEST EXAMPLE

1 $7^2 = $ _____

- Ⓐ   14
- Ⓑ   49
- Ⓒ   77
- Ⓓ   490

THINK ABOUT THE ANSWER

The correct answer is option B. Multiply 7×7 (7 times itself) to find the answer, 49.

NOW YOU TRY IT

2 $\sqrt{81} = $ _____

- Ⓕ   8
- Ⓖ   8.1
- Ⓗ   9
- Ⓙ   18

Check your answer on page 111.

Review Your Work

If you finish the test before time is up, don't leave! Use every minute allowed to check your work. Quickly make sure that you have answered all the questions. Check your answer sheet for mistakes. Proofread any writing.

Advantage Test Prep Grade 7 © 2005 Creative Teaching Press

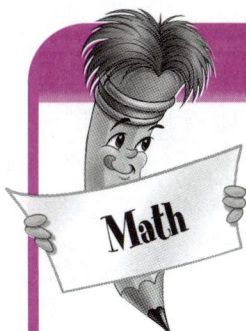

KNOW THE SKILL: ADDING AND SUBTRACTING FRACTIONS WITH UNLIKE DENOMINATORS

In order to add and subtract fractions, the denominators must be the same. To add or subtract fractions with unlike denominators, rewrite them so that they have like denominators. To do this, convert the fraction so that they use the least common denominator (LCD). Think of the multiples of each denominator. The smallest one they have in common is the LCD. For example, to add 1/3 and 1/4, you use the LCD 12. Multiply both the numerator and denominator of 1/3 by 4, and the numerator and denominator of 1/4 by 3. This gives you equivalent fractions with like denominators, 4/12 and 3/12. Then add the numerators to get the answer, 7/12.

DURING THE TEST

Remember that you need to rewrite fractions with unlike denominators using the LCD. Then simplify your answer, if necessary.

TEST EXAMPLE

1 1/6 + 3/8 = _____
- Ⓐ   1/2
- Ⓑ   7/12
- Ⓒ   11/24
- Ⓓ   13/24

THINK ABOUT THE ANSWER

The answer is option D. The LCD for 6 and 8 is 24. Multiply the numerator and denominator of 1/6 by 4 and the numerator and denominator of 3/8 by 3 to get fractions with like denominators of 24 (4/24 and 9/24). Then add the numerators to get 13/24.

NOW YOU TRY IT

2 4/5 – 1/3 = _____
- Ⓕ   7/15
- Ⓖ   1/5
- Ⓗ   9/15
- Ⓙ   2/15

Check your answer on page 111.

Check This Out

Check your answer to an addition problem by subtracting one of the addends from the sum. You should get the other addend. Check your answer to a subtraction problem by adding the difference to the number that you subtracted.

COMPUTATIONS AND OPERATIONS

KNOW THE SKILL: **MULTIPLYING INTEGERS**

Integers are also known as positive and negative numbers. Multiplying two positive numbers gives you a positive product:

$4 \times 2 = 8$

Multiplying two negative numbers also gives you a positive product:

$-4 \times (-2) = 8$

Multiplying a positive and a negative number gives you a negative product:

$4 \times (-2) = -8$

DURING THE TEST

Keep these rules in mind when you are multiplying integers:

If the signs are the same (both positive or both negative) the product is positive.

If the signs are different (one positive, one negative) the product is negative.

TEST EXAMPLE

1 $-6 \times (-3) =$ _____
- Ⓐ 9
- Ⓑ -9
- Ⓒ 18
- Ⓓ -18

THINK ABOUT THE ANSWER

The correct answer is option C. The product of 6 and 3 is 18. Because both numbers have the same sign (negative), the product is a positive number.

NOW YOU TRY IT

2 $4 \times (-5) =$ _____
- Ⓕ 9
- Ⓖ -9
- Ⓗ 20
- Ⓙ -20

Check your answer on page 111.

"Overview" the Test

If it is allowed, quickly flip through the pages of the test so that you will know what lies ahead. This will help you plan your time. Ask whether you can write on the test. If you can, jot notes to yourself. Quickly judge how much time you will need for each part.

Advantage Test Prep Grade 7 © 2005 Creative Teaching Press

Math

KNOW THE SKILL: **DIVIDING DECIMALS**

Dividing decimals is just like dividing whole numbers. The only difference is you must place the decimal correctly. When dividing a decimal by a decimal, move the decimal point of the divisor all the way to the right. Count the number of places the decimal point moved. Then move the decimal point of the dividend the same number of places to the right. Now you can divide by a whole number.

DURING THE TEST

When you are dividing a decimal by a whole number, don't forget to place the decimal point in the quotient right above the decimal point in the dividend.

TEST EXAMPLE

1 4.1 ÷ 0.7 =
- Ⓐ 58.57
- Ⓑ 5.857
- Ⓒ 0.1707
- Ⓓ 0.5857

THINK ABOUT THE ANSWER

The correct answer is option B. Did you remember to move the decimal point in both the dividend and divisor one place to the right? The problem then becomes 41 ÷ 7 = 5.857.

NOW YOU TRY IT

2 0.44 ÷ 9.2 =
- Ⓕ 47.8
- Ⓖ 4.78
- Ⓗ 0.478
- Ⓙ 0.0478

Check your answer on page 111.

Get Testwise

On math questions like these, make sure you always double check the placement of decimal points in numbers.

ESTIMATION AND NUMBER THEORY

KNOW THE SKILL: ESTIMATING TO PREDICT RESULTS

It sometimes happens, in life and on tests, that you don't need an exact answer to a math problem. Estimating also comes in handy when you need to check if your answer to a problem is reasonable. Here are some ways you can use estimating:

- Round numbers to estimate sums, differences, products, and quotients.
- Use front-end estimation to estimate sums and differences.
- Use compatible numbers to estimate sums, differences, products, and quotients.

DURING THE TEST

When you need to estimate or predict an answer on a test:

- Read the problem carefully to decide which operation you need to use.
- Choose a suitable estimation method.
- Estimate the answer.
- Eliminate choices that are not close to the estimate.
- Finally, find the right answer.

TEST EXAMPLE

1 The product of 119 x 3.09 is about _____.

- Ⓐ 36
- Ⓑ 3.6
- Ⓒ 360
- Ⓓ 3,600

THINK ABOUT THE ANSWER

The correct answer is option C. Find the correct estimate by rounding 119 to 120 and 3.09 to 3. Then multiply 120 x 3 to get 360.

NOW YOU TRY IT

2 Estimate an answer for this division problem: 9,016 ÷ 31.

- Ⓕ 30
- Ⓗ 300
- Ⓖ 40
- Ⓙ 400

Check your answer on page 111.

Get Simple

If a problem seems complicated, try replacing the numbers with simpler ones. Then reread the problem, substituting the simpler numbers. When you solve the problem using the simpler numbers, you'll then know how to attack the original problem with the complicated numbers.

Advantage Test Prep Grade 7 © 2005 Creative Teaching Press

KNOW THE SKILL: GREATEST COMMON FACTOR

The greatest common factor is the largest number that is a common factor of two or more numbers. To find the GCF of any two numbers, list all of the factors of each number. The factors that are in each number's list are common factors. The largest of these is the GCF.

DURING THE TEST

In order to find all the factors of any number, think of the factors in pairs. When two numbers are multiplied to equal the number you are factoring, each is a factor of that number. Here are the factor pairs for the number 60: 1 and 60, 2 and 30, 3 and 20, 4 and 15, 5 and 12, and 6 and 10.

TEST EXAMPLE

1 The greatest common factor of 60 and 84 is _____.
- Ⓐ 3
- Ⓑ 6
- Ⓒ 12
- Ⓓ 30

THINK ABOUT THE ANSWER

Option C is correct. Option D is not a factor of 84. Options A, B, and C are common factors of 60 and 84. Of these, 12 is the greatest.

NOW YOU TRY IT

2 6 is the greatest common factor of _____.
- Ⓕ 8 and 12
- Ⓖ 12 and 30
- Ⓗ 12 and 36
- Ⓙ 24 and 56

Check your answer on page 111.

Talk to Your Teacher

Ask your teacher to talk about any problems students have had with the test in the past. Your teacher might know things that will help you. He or she might have advice that can help you get through difficult parts of the test.

KNOW THE SKILL: PRIME FACTORIZATION

A prime number is a counting number that has only two factors, itself and 1. Some prime numbers are 2, 3, 5, 7, and 11. A composite number is a counting number greater than 1 that has more than two factors. Any composite number can be written as the product of prime numbers. This factorization is called the **prime factorization** of the number.

DURING THE TEST

Any time that you are asked to find the prime factorization of an even number, you know that one of the prime factors must be 2. Keep in mind that all the factors in a prime factorization must be prime numbers.

TEST EXAMPLE

1 The prime factorization of 84 is
- Ⓐ $2^2 \times 3 \times 7$
- Ⓑ $2^3 \times 7$
- Ⓒ $3 \times 4 \times 7$
- Ⓓ $3^2 \times 7$

THINK ABOUT THE ANSWER

The answer is option A. Options A and C show factorizations of 84, but only option A shows the prime factorization. Option B shows the prime factorization of 56. Option D shows the prime factorization for 63. Notice that it does not contain 2 or a power of two. It is the prime factorization for an odd number.

NOW YOU TRY IT

2 $2^3 \times 5^2$ is the prime factorization of _____.
- Ⓕ 10
- Ⓗ 100
- Ⓖ 40
- Ⓙ 200

Check your answer on page 111.

Let's Get Together

Form a small study group with members of your class. You can prepare for tests together. After tests you can brainstorm new preparation strategies as a group.

KNOW THE SKILL: AREA OF AN IRREGULAR TWO-DIMENSIONAL FIGURE

Tests may ask you to find the area of oddly-shaped figures that are drawn on a grid.

DURING THE TEST

Be sure to look for the scale, which will tell you the area that each square on the grid represents. Then count the number of complete squares and partial squares that the figure takes up.

TEST EXAMPLE

1 What is the area of the shaded figure?

Ⓐ   7.5 square units

Ⓑ   8 square units

Ⓒ   8.5 square units

Ⓓ   9 square units

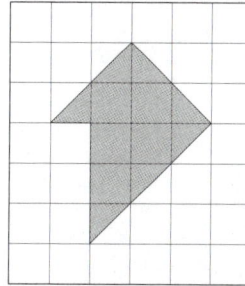

THINK ABOUT THE ANSWER

The correct answer is option C. Count up the number of completely shaded units (5) and the number of half-shaded units (7). The half-shaded units add up to 3.5 square units. Add the totals together to get 8.5 square units as the area.

NOW YOU TRY IT

2 What is the area of the shaded figure?

Ⓕ   7.5 square units

Ⓖ   8 square units

Ⓗ   8.5 square units

Ⓙ   9 square units

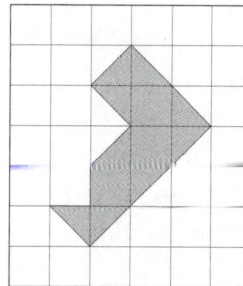

Check your answer on page 111.

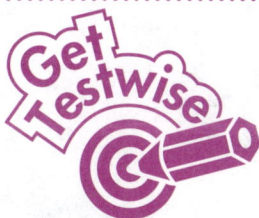

Get Testwise

Tick, Tick, Tick

When counting up units, as in these problems, go ahead and make tick marks on the test page so you'll make sure you don't count a square twice or miss one completely.

KNOW THE SKILL: VOLUME OF A SOLID

The volume of a three-dimensional figure is the measurement of the space inside it.
You will need to memorize these formulas for finding the volumes of different solids
The answers are always in cubic units.

cube: $V = s^3$ rectangular prism: $V = lwh$

DURING THE TEST

If a drawing is not provided, you may want to do a quick sketch of the solid on scratch paper. You can write in the values given to help you better see the figure.

TEST EXAMPLE

1 What is the volume of this solid?

Ⓐ 33 in³
Ⓑ 66 in³
Ⓒ 168 in³
Ⓓ 1,176 in³

12 in
14 in   7 in

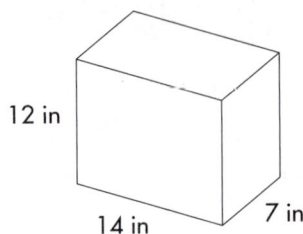

THINK ABOUT THE ANSWER

Option D is correct. This solid is a rectangular prism. Inserting the measurements of the solid into the correct formula gives the equation 12 x 14 x 7 = 1,176 cubic inches.

NOW YOU TRY IT

2 What is the volume of a cube with sides measuring 72 centimeters?

Ⓕ 216 cubic centimeters
Ⓖ 5,184 cubic centimeters
Ⓗ 51,840 cubic centimeters
Ⓙ 373,348 cubic centimeters

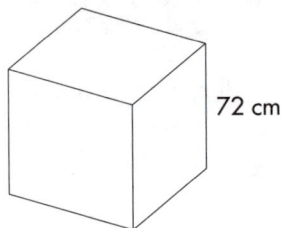

72 cm

Check your answer on page 111.

Get Testwise

Neatness Matters
If your 3s look like 8s, you'll have a big problem on a test. Anyone grading the test needs to be able to read your handwriting. Take the time to write legibly.

KNOW THE SKILL: **SURFACE AREA OF A THREE-DIMENSIONAL FIGURE**

The surface area of a solid is different from the volume, which is the amount of space inside the solid. The surface area is the sum of the areas of all the shapes that cover the outside surface. Think of a cube. Its surface area is the sum of the areas of the six squares that make up its sides. The surface area of a rectangular prism is the sum of the areas of the six squares or rectangles that make up its outside.

DURING THE TEST

A quick way to determine the surface area of a cube is to multiply the square of one side by 6. This works because all the sides of a cube are identical. It won't work with a rectangular prism because its sides are not identical. You'll need to figure out each of the sides' areas separately.

TEST EXAMPLE

1 What is the surface area of this solid?
- Ⓐ 150 square inches
- Ⓑ 30 square inches
- Ⓒ 25 square inches
- Ⓓ 15 square inches

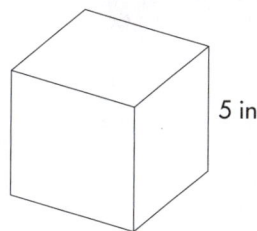

5 in

THINK ABOUT THE ANSWER

The correct answer is option A. To find the surface area of the cube, multiply 5 x 5 to get the area of one side (25 square inches). Then multiply 25 x 6 to get 150 square inches.

NOW YOU TRY IT

2 What is the surface area of this solid?
- Ⓕ 108 cm²
- Ⓖ 180 cm²
- Ⓗ 216 cm²
- Ⓙ 432 cm²

6 cm   10 cm

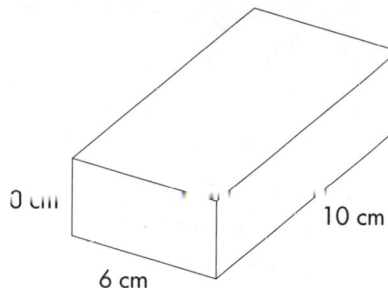

Check your answer on page 111.

Work Quickly

Plan your time, and work quickly through each section of the test. Do not linger on a section if you are done with it. Move on to the next section. Work quickly, but not so quickly that you make mistakes.

KNOW THE SKILL: PYTHAGOREAN RELATIONSHIP

A triangle is a figure with three sides. When one of the angles of a triangle is a right, or 90°, angle, the triangle is called a **right triangle**. The shorter sides, or legs, of a right triangle are usually referred to as *a* and *b*. The side called *c*, which is the side opposite the right angle, is always the longest. Another name for this longest side is the **hypotenuse**. A formula, known as the **Pythagorean Theorem**, shows the relationship between the lengths of the legs and hypotenuse:

$$a^2 + b^2 = c^2$$

DURING THE TEST

Always look for the right angle symbol in a triangle. That way, you'll know it is a right triangle and which side is the hypotenuse.

TEST EXAMPLE

1 What is the length of side *c* in this triangle?
- Ⓐ 10 in
- Ⓑ 14 in
- Ⓒ 36 in
- Ⓓ 64 in

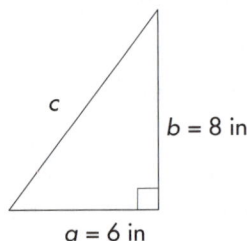

c *b* = 8 in *a* = 6 in

THINK ABOUT THE ANSWER

The correct answer is option A. To find it, use the values of 6 for *a* and 8 for *b* in the Pythagorean Theorem. The equation becomes $6^2 + 8^2 = c^2$. $6^2 = 36$. $8^2 = 64$. $36 + 64 = 100$. Therefore, side $c = \sqrt{100}$, or 10.

NOW YOU TRY IT

2 What is the length of side *b* in this triangle?
- Ⓕ 11 cm
- Ⓖ 12 cm
- Ⓗ 13 cm
- Ⓙ 24 cm

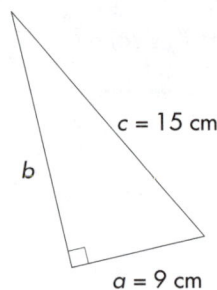

c = 15 cm *b* *a* = 9 cm

Check your answer on page 111.

Get Testwise

Dress Comfortably

Some classrooms are warm and some are cool. Consider dressing in layers. That way you can be comfortable no matter what the conditions.

Advantage Test Prep Grade 7 © 2005 Creative Teaching Press

GEOMETRY

KNOW THE SKILL: CONGRUENCE AND SIMILARITY

When two figures are congruent, they have the same size and shape. The corresponding sides and the corresponding angles are congruent. When two figures are similar, they have the same shape, but not necessarily the same size. The corresponding sides are in proportion, and the corresponding angles are congruent.

DURING THE TEST

A test may ask you to identify congruent or similar triangles or other polygons. You may also be asked to select corresponding angles or sides of congruent or similar figures.

TEST EXAMPLE

1 Which pair of figures is NOT congruent?

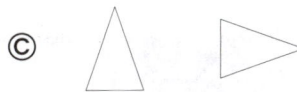

Ⓐ

Ⓒ

Ⓑ

Ⓓ

THINK ABOUT THE ANSWER

The answer is option D. These two polygons are similar, but not congruent. All the other pairs are the same size and shape.

NOW YOU TRY IT

2 These figures are similar. Which angle corresponds to angle C?

Ⓕ   angle W
Ⓖ   angle X
Ⓗ   angle Y
Ⓙ   angle Z

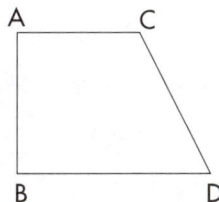

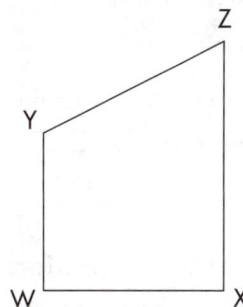

Check your answer on page 111.

Advantage Test Prep Grade 7 © 2005 Creative Teaching Press

69

MATHEMATICS: GEOMETRY

KNOW THE SKILL: EXAMINING SHAPES ON A COORDINATE GRID

Slides, flips, and turns describe different ways to move shapes on a grid. They are also known as transformations. The form and size of the shapes do not change when they are transformed. Only the position of the shapes changes.

DURING THE TEST

Shapes are often drawn on a grid, making it easier to work with transformations. A test may ask you to slide, flip, or turn a shape drawn on a grid. Keep these definitions in mind:

- A slide is the motion of a shape along a line. You can think of the way a drawer opens. The position of the drawer changes, but its shape does not.
- A flipped shape takes on the shape of its own reflection across a line. Think of the lower-case letters *b* and *d*. When a *d* is flipped, it looks like a *b*.
- A turned shape is rotated around a single point. If a *d* is rotated around the point at the top of the part that sticks up so that it is upside-down, it will look like a *p*.

TEST EXAMPLE

1 If this shape is turned on point A 180° clockwise, what will it look like?

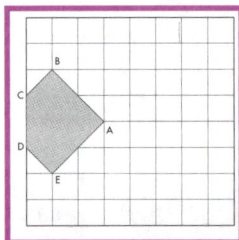 Ⓐ 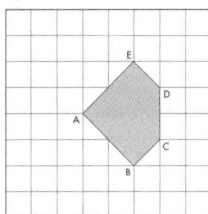 Ⓑ 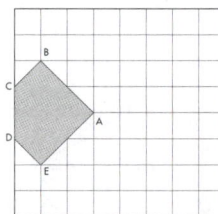 Ⓒ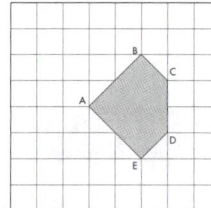

THINK ABOUT THE ANSWER

The answer is option C. It has been turned 180° clockwise on point A. Option B has not been moved. Option C has been rotated, and also flipped..

NOW YOU TRY IT

2 If this shape is flipped across line *AJ*, what will it look like?

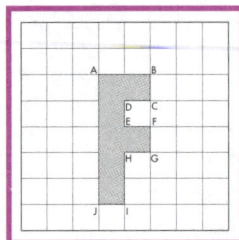 Ⓕ 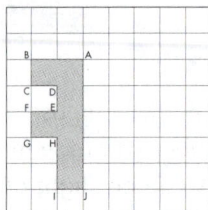 Ⓖ 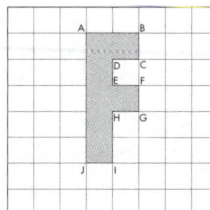 Ⓗ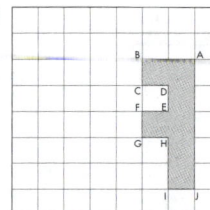

Check your answer on page 111.

Advantage Test Prep Grade 7 © 2005 Creative Teaching Press

KNOW THE SKILL: **EVALUATING EXPRESSIONS**

In an expression or equation, letters can stand for unknown numbers. These letters are known as **variables**. When we replace a variable with a specific number and then perform the operations, it is called **evaluating the expression**. To evaluate the expression $2x + 4x$, where $x = 4$, begin by replacing each letter with its assigned value:

$$2(4) + 4(4)$$

Then do the operations from left to right, first multiplying, then adding:

$$2(4) + 4(4) = 8 + 16 = 24$$

DURING THE TEST

Always do math operations in the following order: First, do operations inside parentheses. Then perform all multiplications and divisions from left to right. Then do all additions and subtractions from left to right.

TEST EXAMPLE

1 What is the value of the expression $5n - 3$ if $n = 4$?
- Ⓐ 5
- Ⓑ 12
- Ⓒ 17
- Ⓓ 20

THINK ABOUT THE ANSWER

The correct answer is option C. Here's how to evaluate this expression when n = 4:
$5(4) - 3 = 20 - 3 = 17$.

NOW YOU TRY IT

2 What is the value of the expression $3n + 4n$ if $n = 5$?
- Ⓕ 7
- Ⓖ 15
- Ⓗ 20
- Ⓙ 35

Check your answer on page 111.

Get Testwise

What Does That Mean?
If you forget the meaning of a math term, use the word in a different context. For example, if you can't remember what the math term *variable* means, think about the word *weather*. Winds can be "light and variable." In this sentence, *variable* means "changing." In math, a variable is a symbol that can have changing values.

KNOW THE SKILL: SOLVING EQUATIONS WITH ONE VARIABLE

An equation is a mathematical sentence that shows that two expressions are equal. An equation often has a variable in it. To solve an equation for the variable, you need to get the variable alone on one side of the equation. Do this by using inverse operations. Addition and subtraction are inverse operations. Multiplication and division are inverse operations.

DURING THE TEST

You may be asked to find the value of a variable in an equation. You may also be asked to write an equation based on information given. Finally, a test may require you to choose an equation that represents information in a story problem.

TEST EXAMPLE

1 Solve for the variable y in the equation $8y = 56$.

    Ⓐ   4
    Ⓑ   5
    Ⓒ   6
    Ⓓ   7

THINK ABOUT THE ANSWER

The correct answer is option D. To get the variable alone on one side of the equation, use the inverse operation of multiplication, which is division. Divide each side of the equation by 8 to get $y = 7$.

NOW YOU TRY IT

2 Which equation does NOT have a solution of 12?

    Ⓕ $4x = 48$
    Ⓖ $24 \div x = 2$
    Ⓗ $x - 3 = 9$
    Ⓙ $4 + x = 18$

Check your answer on page 111

Get Testwise

Check It Out
Always check your answer by replacing the value you find for the variable in the original equation. In question 1 above, check your answer by rewriting the equation as $8(7) = 56$.

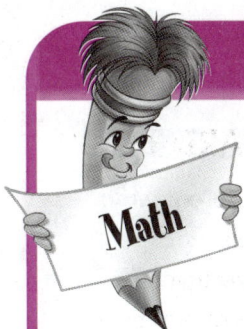

KNOW THE SKILL: GRAPHING LINEAR EQUATIONS

The value of variables in an equation can be shown on a graph. The graph consists of two crossed lines called axes. The x-axis is horizontal. The y-axis is vertical. Each axis has a scale, usually 1, 2, 3, 4, and so on. The point where they meet has a value of 0,0. This means zero on the horizontal x-axis and zero on the vertical y-axis. A point on the graph represents a value for each variable. A linear equation is an equation whose solution is a straight line on the graph.

The graph at the right shows the line for the equation $x = y + 1$. Can you see that each point on the line represents a pair of values that will correctly solve the equation?

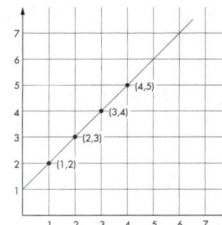

DURING THE TEST

To find points on a graph that will solve an equation, start by assigning a value to x, then solve to find the value of y. Find this point. Assign the next higher value to x and solve again. This will give you another point. Because the equation is linear, a straight line drawn through these two points will give you a set of points, each of which will solve the equation.

TEST EXAMPLE

1 Which equation does the graph show?

- Ⓐ $x = 2y$
- Ⓑ $2x = y$
- Ⓒ $x = y$
- Ⓓ $x = y \div 2$

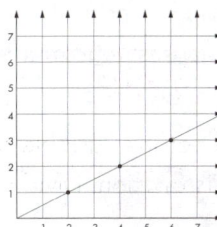

THINK ABOUT THE ANSWER

Option A is correct. Replacing the variables in the equation with the values represented by the points correctly solves the equation. For example, the first set of points is 2,1 (that is $x = 2$ and $y = 1$). These values give you an equation of $2 = 2(1)$, or $2 = 2$.

NOW YOU TRY IT

2 Which graph shows the equation $x \div 3 = y$?

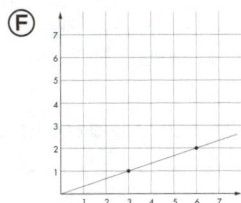

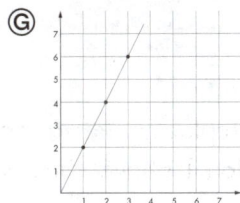

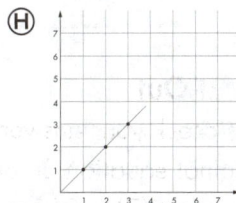

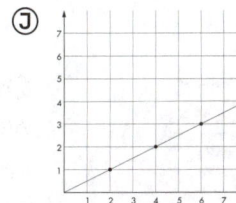

Ⓕ   Ⓖ   Ⓗ   Ⓙ

Check your answer on page 111.

KNOW THE SKILL: **FINDING MEASURES OF CENTER AND SPREAD**

A measure of center is a value at the center of a set of data. There are different ways to find the center of a data set.

- The most common is the **mean**. Many people call the mean an **average**. To find the mean, add all the values in the data set. Then divide the sum by the number of values.
- Another measure of center is the **median**. To find the median, arrange all the data points in order, The value in the middle is the median.
- The **mode** is the value that occurs most often.
- The difference between the two greatest values in a data set is called the **range**. The range is a measure of spread.

DURING THE TEST

Tests may ask you to find any of these measures of center or spread. Make sure you know which one you're being asked to calculate.

TEST EXAMPLE

1 Martina received the following scores on her math tests: 91, 93, 88, 95, 88, and 84. What is her mean score, rounded to the nearest whole number?

   Ⓐ 91   Ⓒ 89

   Ⓑ 90   Ⓓ 88

THINK ABOUT THE ANSWER

The correct answer is option B. Adding the six scores and dividing by 6 gives you 89.833, Round the answer up to 90.

NOW YOU TRY IT

2 The high temperatures during one week were 63, 69, 55, 52, 55, 59, and 61 degrees. What was the range of the temperatures?

   Ⓕ 69   Ⓗ 55

   Ⓖ 59   Ⓙ 17

Check your answer on page 111.

Step by Step

When using more than one operation to solve a problem, such as adding the values in a data set, then dividing by the number of values, work in steps. Do one operation at a time.

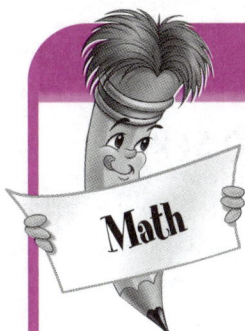

KNOW THE SKILL: COMPUTING PROBABILITIES FOR SIMPLE AND COMPOUND EVENTS

Probability is the chance that an event will happen. For example, if you flip a coin, what are the chances you will get heads? You can compute the probability of this event happening this way:

$$\frac{\text{Successful outcomes (getting heads)}}{\text{All possible outcomes (getting heads or tails)}} = \frac{1}{2}$$

The probability of getting heads is 1/2. Probability is expressed as a fraction. 1 means that an event is certain to happen, while 0 means that an event is certain not to happen. The probability of getting either a heads or a tails is 1. The probability of getting neither a heads nor a tails is 0, since one or the other has to happen.

DURING THE TEST

You may be asked to compute the probability of two events happening, called a **compound event**. For example, what is the probability of flipping two coins and getting two heads? Find the probability of a compound event this way:

- Find the probability of one event happening (getting 1 heads) = 1/2
- Find the probability of the other event happening (getting 1 heads) = 1/2
- Multiply the two fractions that represent the probability of each event happening
  1/2 x 1/2 = 1/4

The probability of flipping two coins and getting heads on both flips is 1/4.

TEST EXAMPLE

1. A game spinner is divided into 5 equal sections: red, yellow, green, blue, and brown. What is the probability that you will get a blue and then a brown on two spins?

   Ⓐ 1/5   Ⓒ 2/25

   Ⓑ 2/5   Ⓓ 1/25

THINK ABOUT THE ANSWER

The answer is option D. To find it, compute the probability for getting a blue on your first spin (1/5). Then find the probability for getting a brown on your second spin (also 1/5). Multiply the two probabilities to get 1/25. These are the chances that you will get a blue and a brown on consecutive spins.

NOW YOU TRY IT

2. Look at this spinner. What is the probability that you will spin a dog, then a cat?

   Ⓕ 1/8   Ⓗ 1/2

   Ⓖ 1/4   Ⓙ 2/3

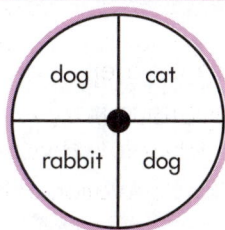

Check your answer on page 111.

KNOW THE SKILL: **REPRESENTING DATA GRAPHICALLY**

It is often easier and clearer to represent data in a graph, rather than in words. A **graph** is a kind of drawing that shows how different numbers relate to each other. For example, think of a **pie chart**, in which a circle is divided in different size "pieces of pie" that show different amounts or values. A **line graph** can show how values change over time, such as how the average daily temperature goes up and down over a month.

DURING THE TEST

A bar graph shows the relative sizes of different sets of data. A larger or taller column or bar represents a higher value or number of the things being compared than a smaller one.

TEST EXAMPLE

1 Look at this bar graph. It shows the number of students who chose different colors as their favorite. Ten students chose red, four chose blue, five picked green, four picked purple, and two chose orange. Which bars represent blue and purple?

Favorite Colors

    Ⓐ   3 and 5

    Ⓑ   3 and 4

    Ⓒ   1 and 2

    Ⓓ   2 and 4

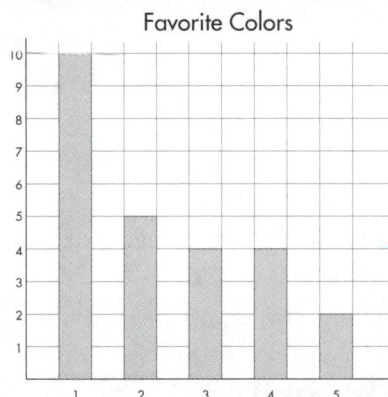

THINK ABOUT THE ANSWER

The correct answer is option B. Because a bar graph shows the relationship of different values to each other, the largest bar represents red. The second largest represents green. The third and fourth bars, which are the same size, represent blue and purple. Each had four students chose it as their favorite color.

NOW YOU TRY IT

2 A bar graph shows the grades, A to F, that class members received on a math test. Which of the following statements is true about the bar graph?

    Ⓕ   The largest bar will represent the grade that the largest number of students received.

    Ⓖ   The smallest bar will represent the grade that the largest number of students received.

    Ⓗ   The largest bar will represent the number of students who received Bs.

    Ⓙ   The largest bar will represent the number of students who received As.

Check your answer on page 112.

Advantage Test Prep Grade 7 © 2005 Creative Teaching Press

KNOW THE SKILL: SOLVING A MULTI-STEP PROBLEM

Follow these steps to solve a word problem:
1. Read the problem carefully.
2. Analyze the information given.
3. Make a plan for solving the problem.
4. Do the math and check your answer.

DURING THE TEST

Tests may ask you to solve problems that involve more than one step to find the correct answer. The two problems on this page are examples of multi-step problems. You may find it helpful to write on scratch paper to make clear the two parts of the problem.

TEST EXAMPLE

1 Sarah and Corrine are saving up to buy a lamb to show at their county fair. Sarah has saved $32, and Corrine has saved $27. If the lamb costs $110, how much more do they need to save to buy the lamb?

  Ⓐ $15   Ⓒ $51
  Ⓑ $25   Ⓓ $59

THINK ABOUT THE ANSWER

The answer is option C. First you have to determine how much the girls have saved together. The sum of $32 and $27 is $59. Then subtract the amount they have already saved together from the cost of the lamb: $110 − $59 = $51.

NOW YOU TRY IT

2 Erin is in charge of buying paint for the church basement. A gallon can of paint costs $23.55. If she buys a dozen cans, she will be charged $235.16. How much of a discount will she receive if she buys a dozen cans?

  Ⓕ 5%   Ⓗ 17%
  Ⓖ 12%   Ⓙ 41%

Check your answer on page 112.

Watch Your Units

In word problems like these, make sure your answer is in the correct units. For example, your answer to problem 2 needs to be a percent, not a dollar amount.

Math

KNOW THE SKILL: **SOLVING A PROPORTION PROBLEM**

A **ratio** is a comparison of two numbers. The two numbers are usually separated by a colon. An example is 2:3. This ratio can also be written 2/3. Either way, we say the ratio is "two to three." A proportion is an equation with a ratio on each side.

DURING THE TEST

A test may ask you to find an unknown number in one of the ratios of a proportion. Often you will have to set up the equation from a story problem. Use cross products to find the number, a procedure known as solving a proportion. For example, here's how to use cross products to solve the proportion $2/3 = n/9$:

> $3 \times n = 2 \times 9$, or $3n = 18$. Divide each side by 3 to isolate the variable on one side. This leaves $n = 6$. The missing number in the proportion is 6: $2/3 = 6/9$. Say "Two is to three as six is to nine."

TEST EXAMPLE

1 Which number correctly completes the proportion $3/8 = 6/n$?

   Ⓐ   8   Ⓒ   24

   Ⓑ 16   Ⓓ 48

THINK ABOUT THE ANSWER

The answer is option B. Using cross products, $3 \times n = 6 \times 8$, or $3n = 48$. Divide each side by 3 to isolate the variable on one side. This leaves $n = 16$. The missing number in the proportion is 16: $3/8 = 6/16$.

NOW YOU TRY IT

2 Rewrite the ratios $2:n$ and $40:100$ as a proportion and solve for the missing number.

   Ⓕ   200

   Ⓖ   40

   Ⓗ   20

   Ⓙ   5

Check your answer on page 112.

Get Testwise

Not the Same

Be careful with ratios and proportions. A 2:1 ratio is not the same as a 1:2 ratio.

Practice Test Introduction

The rest of this book is a practice test. It's like the standardized or proficiency test you might have to take at school. On this practice test, you'll have a chance to use all the skills you've gained by working through the lessons in this book.

The test is divided into the same sections as the earlier parts of the book. There's a test on reading, writing, language, and mathematics. The questions in each test are similar to the ones you've been practicing. Use the answer sheets on the next two pages for answering each test.

Here are some tips to keep in mind as you take the practice tests.

- Don't worry if you're a little nervous. In fact, being a little nervous can sometimes help you to do your best.
- Remember the *Get Testwise* suggestions you read at the bottom of each practice page. They can help you on the practice test, just like they can help you on the real thing.
- Make sure you understand all the directions before you start a test. Ask an adult if you have any questions about the directions.
- Unlike a real standardized test, there's no time limit on this practice test. However, try to work as quickly as you can. Working quickly will give you practice in managing your time.
- If you don't know an answer, you can guess at it or skip it to come back to later.
- Try to complete a whole test, such as the reading test or the math test, at one time. You'll probably want to take a break between tests.
- After finishing each test, check yourself. Use the answer key to each test. You'll find the practice test answers at the very back of the book starting on page 112.

STUDENT INFORMATION SHEET

Complete this student information sheet. It is similar to ones found on tests. Be sure to fill in the correct bubble for each letter of your name.

STUDENT'S NAME

LAST	FIRST	MI	SCHOOL

TEACHER

FEMALE ○   **MALE** ○

BIRTHDATE

MONTH	DAY	YEAR

JAN ○	⓪ ⓪	⓪ ⓪
FEB ○	① ①	① ①
MAR ○	② ②	② ②
APR ○	③ ③	③ ③
MAY ○	④	④ ④
JUN ○	⑤	⑤ ⑤
JUL ○	⑥	⑥ ⑥
AUG ○	⑦	⑦ ⑦
SEP ○	⑧	⑧ ⑧
OCT ○	⑨	⑨ ⑨
NOV ○		
DEC ○		

GRADE

④   ⑤   ⑥   ⑦   ⑧

The name grid contains columns of bubbled letters A through Z for LAST, FIRST, and MI portions of the student's name.

Advantage Test Prep Grade 7 © 2005 Creative Teaching Press

PRACTICE TEST ANSWER SHEET

READING

1. Ⓐ Ⓑ Ⓒ Ⓓ   6. Ⓕ Ⓖ Ⓗ Ⓙ   11. Ⓐ Ⓑ Ⓒ Ⓓ   16. Ⓕ Ⓖ Ⓗ Ⓙ   21. Ⓐ Ⓑ Ⓒ Ⓓ
2. Ⓕ Ⓖ Ⓗ Ⓙ   7. Ⓐ Ⓑ Ⓒ Ⓓ   12. Ⓕ Ⓖ Ⓗ Ⓙ   17. Ⓐ Ⓑ Ⓒ Ⓓ   22. Ⓕ Ⓖ Ⓗ Ⓙ
3. Ⓐ Ⓑ Ⓒ Ⓓ   8. Ⓕ Ⓖ Ⓗ Ⓙ   13. Ⓐ Ⓑ Ⓒ Ⓓ   18. Ⓕ Ⓖ Ⓗ Ⓙ   23. Ⓐ Ⓑ Ⓒ Ⓓ
4. Written answer   9. Ⓐ Ⓑ Ⓒ Ⓓ   14. Ⓕ Ⓖ Ⓗ Ⓙ   19. Ⓐ Ⓑ Ⓒ Ⓓ   24. Ⓕ Ⓖ Ⓗ Ⓙ
5. Ⓐ Ⓑ Ⓒ Ⓓ   10. Written answer   15. Ⓐ Ⓑ Ⓒ Ⓓ   20. Ⓕ Ⓖ Ⓗ Ⓙ

LANGUAGE

25. Ⓐ Ⓑ Ⓒ Ⓓ   31. Ⓐ Ⓑ Ⓒ Ⓓ   37. Ⓐ Ⓑ Ⓒ Ⓓ   43. Ⓐ Ⓑ Ⓒ Ⓓ   49. Ⓐ Ⓑ Ⓒ Ⓓ
26. Ⓕ Ⓖ Ⓗ Ⓙ   32. Ⓕ Ⓖ Ⓗ Ⓙ   38. Ⓕ Ⓖ Ⓗ Ⓙ   44. Ⓕ Ⓖ Ⓗ Ⓙ   50. Ⓕ Ⓖ Ⓗ Ⓙ
27. Ⓐ Ⓑ Ⓒ Ⓓ   33. Ⓐ Ⓑ Ⓒ Ⓓ   39. Ⓐ Ⓑ Ⓒ Ⓓ   45. Ⓐ Ⓑ Ⓒ Ⓓ   51. Ⓐ Ⓑ Ⓒ Ⓓ
28. Ⓕ Ⓖ Ⓗ Ⓙ   34. Ⓕ Ⓖ Ⓗ Ⓙ   40. Ⓕ Ⓖ Ⓗ Ⓙ   46. Ⓕ Ⓖ Ⓗ Ⓙ   52. Ⓕ Ⓖ Ⓗ Ⓙ
29. Ⓐ Ⓑ Ⓒ Ⓓ   35. Ⓐ Ⓑ Ⓒ Ⓓ   41. Ⓐ Ⓑ Ⓒ Ⓓ   47. Ⓐ Ⓑ Ⓒ Ⓓ   53. Ⓐ Ⓑ Ⓒ Ⓓ
30. Ⓕ Ⓖ Ⓗ Ⓙ   36. Ⓕ Ⓖ Ⓗ Ⓙ   42. Ⓕ Ⓖ Ⓗ Ⓙ   48. Ⓕ Ⓖ Ⓗ Ⓙ   54. Ⓕ Ⓖ Ⓗ Ⓙ

MATH

55. Ⓐ Ⓑ Ⓒ Ⓓ   63. Ⓐ Ⓑ Ⓒ Ⓓ   71. Ⓐ Ⓑ Ⓒ Ⓓ   79. Ⓐ Ⓑ Ⓒ Ⓓ   87. Ⓐ Ⓑ Ⓒ Ⓓ
56. Ⓕ Ⓖ Ⓗ Ⓙ   64. Ⓕ Ⓖ Ⓗ Ⓙ   72. Ⓕ Ⓖ Ⓗ Ⓙ   80. Ⓕ Ⓖ Ⓗ Ⓙ   88. Ⓕ Ⓖ Ⓗ Ⓙ
57. Ⓐ Ⓑ Ⓒ Ⓓ   65. Ⓐ Ⓑ Ⓒ Ⓓ   73. Ⓐ Ⓑ Ⓒ Ⓓ   81. Ⓐ Ⓑ Ⓒ Ⓓ   89. Ⓐ Ⓑ Ⓒ Ⓓ
58. Ⓕ Ⓖ Ⓗ Ⓙ   66. Ⓕ Ⓖ Ⓗ Ⓙ   74. Ⓕ Ⓖ Ⓗ Ⓙ   82. Ⓕ Ⓖ Ⓗ Ⓙ   90. Ⓕ Ⓖ Ⓗ Ⓙ
59. Ⓐ Ⓑ Ⓒ Ⓓ   67. Ⓐ Ⓑ Ⓒ Ⓓ   75. Ⓐ Ⓑ Ⓒ Ⓓ   83. Ⓐ Ⓑ Ⓒ Ⓓ   91. Ⓐ Ⓑ Ⓒ Ⓓ
60. Ⓕ Ⓖ Ⓗ Ⓙ   68. Ⓕ Ⓖ Ⓗ Ⓙ   76. Ⓕ Ⓖ Ⓗ Ⓙ   84. Ⓕ Ⓖ Ⓗ Ⓙ   92. Ⓕ Ⓖ Ⓗ Ⓙ
61. Ⓐ Ⓑ Ⓒ Ⓓ   69. Ⓐ Ⓑ Ⓒ Ⓓ   77. Ⓐ Ⓑ Ⓒ Ⓓ   85. Ⓐ Ⓑ Ⓒ Ⓓ   93. Ⓐ Ⓑ Ⓒ Ⓓ
62. Ⓕ Ⓖ Ⓗ Ⓙ   70. Ⓕ Ⓖ Ⓗ Ⓙ   78. Ⓕ Ⓖ Ⓗ Ⓙ   86. Ⓕ Ⓖ Ⓗ Ⓙ   94. Ⓕ Ⓖ Ⓗ Ⓙ

Read the passage, *Into the Skies*. Then answer questions 1 through 10.

Into the Skies

It all started with the discovery of fire. As people gazed wonderingly at campfires and into fireplaces, they noticed something enthralling. You've probably noticed it too. Little bits of ash, paper, and smoke all rise above the fire. Why does this happen, people wondered. Can we use this fact to lift ourselves into the air?

Although it took many centuries, the eventual answer was yes. The people who finally answered the questions were two French brothers, Joseph and Étienne Montgolfier. According to a story told about the brothers, they were watching silk hung up to dry over a warm oven. They saw the sheer silk rise and flutter above the warm air that rose from the oven. The sons of a papermaker, the Montgolfiers had also noticed small bits of paper rising over their family's paper factory.

Armed with this knowledge gained from careful observation, they set out to harness the power that made the silk and paper rise. In experiments, they filled paper and cloth bags with smoke, steam, and hot air. They lit fires and burned different fuels underneath the bags, which were open at the bottom, In all cases, the bags rose.

The brothers concluded that an unknown gas, released from the burning fuel, entered the bags and caused them to begin to float. Even though they were incorrect, their experiments led them in the right direction.

One summer day in 1783, a strange sight greeted the eyes of people in Paris, France. A huge gaily colored bag, made of cloth and paper and held together by buttons, stood in a field. The bag measured 35 feet in diameter, as large as a small house. Its open bottom lay on a platform. On the platform was a pile of wool and straw.

The spectators watched as the Montgolfiers lit the pile on fire. As the smoke rose into the balloon, the great bag filled. Then, to the consternation of the crowd, it swiftly rose to an incredible height. One observer estimated it reached 6,000 feet! After ten minutes of flight, it dropped back to the ground and disappeared in a great blaze.

Now that the Montgolfiers knew their invention would fly, they decided to send up some passengers in a basket attached to the bottom of the balloon. Even the king heard about their exciting break-through. He asked them to launch a balloon from one of his palaces. A few weeks later, another balloon was prepared. The brothers were unsure that people could breathe the air at such a great height, so the honor of being the first to fly went to a rooster, a duck, and a sheep! Again, the experiment was a success, and the passengers returned safe and sound. The only injury occurred when the sheep stepped on the rooster's wing.

Finally, the Montgolfiers were ready for human passengers. On October 15, 1783, a friend climbed into the balloon's basket. He rose 84 feet above the ground, anchored to the earth by a long rope. The climax of the Montgolfiers' balloon experiments occurred a few months later. A beautiful blue and gold balloon, unattached to the ground, soared 5 miles in 25 minutes, reaching an altitude of 500 feet. Two passengers enjoyed the spectacular view. One of the awed spectators that day was Benjamin Franklin.

The brothers' only error was thinking that an unknown "lifting" gas raised their balloons. In fact, it was hot air. They could have burned anything. In spite of this miscalculation, they are known as the first pioneers of hot-air ballooning.

GO →

1 Read the sentence from the selection. Which word does NOT mean the same as *enthralling*?

As people gazed wonderingly at campfires and into fireplaces, they noticed something enthralling.

Ⓐ intriguing   Ⓒ motivating

Ⓑ fascinating   Ⓓ captivating

2 The Montgolfiers waited to send a human passenger up in their balloon because _____.

Ⓕ They saw silk rise and flutter above the warm air that rose from an oven.

Ⓖ They feared people might not be able to breathe the air at higher altitudes.

Ⓗ The king asked them to send up a rooster, a duck, and a sheep.

Ⓙ Their theories about why the balloons rose were incorrect.

3 Which of the following is a generalization you could draw from the selection about the Montgolfiers?

Ⓐ Scientists rarely make mistakes.

Ⓑ Few people are interested in flying.

Ⓒ Being wrong about the cause of a phenomenon will derail any experiment.

Ⓓ It is prudent to be cautious when doing experiments that could be dangerous.

4 Imagine you were asked to make a time line of the events described in the selection about the Montgolfiers. Place the following events in the correct time order: the French king asks them to launch a balloon from his palace; Montgolfiers watch bits of paper float up the factory chimney; Benjamin Franklin watches their demonstration flight; the brothers conclude that an unknown gas makes bags rise; they send animals up in a balloon.

_____

_____

_____

5 Read the following sentence from the story.

In spite of this miscalculation, they are known as the first pioneers of hot-air ballooning.

What is the meaning of the prefix *mis-*, as used in the word *miscalculation*?

Ⓐ half   Ⓒ bad, wrong

Ⓑ after   Ⓓ together with

GO ➡

6 *Sheer* is to *silk* as _____ is to *iron*.
- Ⓕ metallic
- Ⓖ useful
- Ⓗ heavy
- Ⓙ dark

7 What can you infer about the attitude of the French king towards the Montgolfiers' experiments?
- Ⓐ He felt intrigued by them.
- Ⓑ He felt protective of them.
- Ⓒ He felt hostile toward them.
- Ⓓ He felt indifferent toward them.

8 Read the sentence from the selection. Which word or words mean the same as *harness*?

Armed with this knowledge, gained from careful observation, they set out to harness the power that made the silk and paper rise.

- Ⓕ bother
- Ⓖ bring under control
- Ⓗ straps for climbing gear
- Ⓙ fitting for horse or other animal

9 Imagine that you have been asked to conduct an experiment to prove that hot air makes a bag rise. Which of the following steps would you take first?
- Ⓐ Measure how high the bag rises.
- Ⓑ Light a small fire underneath the bag.
- Ⓒ Build a small fire underneath the bag.
- Ⓓ Prepare a paper or cloth bag with a hole in the bottom.

10 Which of the following graphic aids would be most useful to illustrate a magazine article about the Montgolfier brothers and their experiments: map, line graph, pie chart, time line. Why?

_____

_____

_____

GO

The Story of the Bat

—a Zapotec myth

Long ago, when Light and Darkness were new, the bat looked exactly like he does today. His name meant the bare-winged butterfly. He was the ugliest—and the saddest—creature of all the creatures in the world.

One especially cold day, the bat was shivering. He decided to flap his leathery wings and fly up to heaven. He found God and said to him, "I am freezing. Could I have just a few feathers?" But God had a rule that he would never change the creatures that he had made. He had no feathers for the bat. "Go back on down to the world," God said, "and ask each of the birds to give you a single feather. And remember to be humble about these gifts."

The bat flew back down to the world. He decided to look for the birds with the most beautiful feathers. He received a bright green feather from the parrot. He received a deep blue feather from the pigeon. He received a pure white feather from the dove. He even received an iridescent feather from the tiny hummingbird that shimmered in the sunlight.

All of these gorgeous feathers, and many more as well, the bat received from the birds. When he put them on, he was so proud of his new beauty that he flew all day long. When the first rays of the morning sun struck his new feathers, the bat almost burst with happiness and pride. The others birds stared at him. They had to admit that the bat was certainly striking. He combined all their different beauties into one overwhelming beauty.

At dawn and dusk, the bat's beauty turned the sky a fiery red. Sometimes he was even able to fly across the sky in a great curve just after a rainstorm. Then, he would leave a colored path that contained all the colors of his many feathers.

Sometimes, when he knew the birds were watching, the bat would sit on a tree branch, cleaning his wings and drying them off. He would spread them out as far as he could, so they would catch the light and heat of the sun. At these times, the bat's pride in his feathers became too much for the other birds. To see him sitting there, the most beautiful creature in the world, made them sorry they had donated their feathers. They began to grumble.

It was the hummingbird who came up with the plan. "Let's fly up to God," she suggested. "We'll tell him what the bat is doing." A large flock of birds, comprising all the birds who had given feathers to the bat, winged their way up to heaven.

"You've go to do something about the bat," they cried. "He's making fun of us."

"Besides," added the hummingbird, "we're cold because we have one less feather to keep us warm."

God thought for a while. Then he asked the birds to send the bat to him.

When the bat arrived, God asked him to show him what he had been doing to make the other birds jealous. The bat unfurled his wings and showed off his feathers. The bat's extreme pride angered God. When the bat started to flap his wings to make his feathers shimmer, they all started to fall off! In just a few shakes, his wings and little body were as naked and leathery as they had been. People say that it rained beautiful feathers from the skies for a whole day.

That's why today the bat flies alone and at night. Some say he is diving for his lost feathers. And he never stops, because he wants no one to see his ugliness.

GO

11 Which answer best describes the birds' motivation for asking God to do something about the bat?

    Ⓐ   They are afraid of the bat.

    Ⓑ   They are cold without their feathers.

    Ⓒ   They are angry at God for helping the bat.

    Ⓓ   They are angry at themselves and jealous of the bat.

12 Read the sentence from the selection. Which word or words mean the same as *comprising*?

A large flock of birds, comprising all the birds who had given feathers to the bat, winged their way up to heaven.

    Ⓕ   except for

    Ⓖ   composing

    Ⓗ   made up of

    Ⓙ   in addition to

13 What do we call the curved, colored path the bat made with his feathers?

    Ⓐ   sunset

    Ⓑ   rainbow

    Ⓒ   thundercloud

    Ⓓ   northern lights

14 *Iridescent* is to *shimmer* as _____ is to *shatter*.

    Ⓕ   complicated

    Ⓖ   expensive

    Ⓗ   ceramic

    Ⓙ   brittle

15 Which of the following is the effect of the bat's excessive pride in his feathers?

    Ⓐ   He was able to leave a colored path in the sky.

    Ⓑ   The birds flew up to God to complain.

    Ⓒ   He asks God to help him keep warm.

    Ⓓ   The birds got cold more easily.

GO →

16 Which of these plot events happened first?

    (F)   The bat decided to look for the most beautiful feathers.

    (G)   The bat flew up to heaven to tell God he was cold.

    (H)   The hummingbird thinks up a plan.

    (J)   It rains feathers for an entire day.

17 Which answer best describes the conflict between the two different parts of the bat's personality?

    (A)   He knows he should obey God, but his pride in his new beauty is too great.

    (B)   He wants the birds to like him, but they become envious of him.

    (C)   He wants to be warm, but he also wants new, beautiful feathers.

    (D)   He can't decide which of his new feathers is the most beautiful.

18 What conclusion can you draw about why the Zapotec people told this story?

    (F)   They wanted to show that God is powerful.

    (G)   They hoped God would make the bat beautiful again.

    (H)   They wanted to explain why birds have beautiful feathers.

    (J)   They wanted an explanation for why the bat looks and behaves like it does.

19 Which line from the story might be an example of foreshadowing?

    (A)   And remember to be humble about these gifts.

    (B)   He decided to look for the birds with the most beautiful feathers.

    (C)   But God had a rule that he would never change the creatures that he had made.

    (D)   He was the ugliest—and the saddest—creature of all the creatures in the world.

20 What object or objects in the myth might be a symbol for excessive pride, which can lead to a downfall?

    (F)   the bat

    (G)   the rainbow

    (H)   the white feather

    (J)   the hummingbird

GO

21 About how many years passed between the first and the last events shown on the time line?

1926	Robert Goddard launches first liquid-fuel rockets.
1957	Soviet Union launches *Sputnik*, the first satellite.
1961	Yuri Gagarin becomes first human to travel in space.
1962	John Glenn becomes first American to orbit the earth.
1969	Neil Armstrong walks on the moon.
1971	Soviets place first space station in orbit.
1986	Space shuttle *Challenger* explodes on take-off.
1990	Hubble Space Telescope launched into orbit
1997	*Pathfinder* probe lands on Mars.
2000	First crew arrives at International Space Station.
2003	Space shuttle *Columbia* breaks apart.

    Ⓐ   about 50   Ⓒ   about 90

    Ⓑ   about 75   Ⓓ   about 110

22 Which would you use to show graphically the temperature at different times during a single day?

    Ⓕ   map   Ⓗ   pie chart

    Ⓖ   index   Ⓙ   line graph

23 Read the dictionary entry and answer the question.

a•vi•an (ã ve en) *adj.* Of, relating to, or characteristic of birds. — [From Latin *avis*, bird. See awi in Appendix.]

What part of speech is this word?

    Ⓐ   noun   Ⓒ   adverb

    Ⓑ   verb   Ⓓ   adjective

24 Look at the pie chart. Then answer the question.

How many planes does Sky-Ways operate that are NOT 747s?

    Ⓕ   12

    Ⓖ   57

    Ⓗ   69

    Ⓙ   175

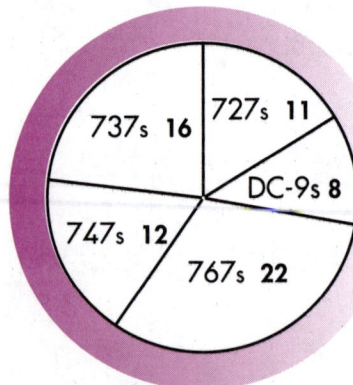

STOP

Writing Prompt

Imagine that a classmate who has never been to your home is going to visit after school. Think about the best way for this person to get to your home. Write several paragraphs giving exact directions from school to your home. If the classmate will be walking, include information like street names, buildings and other landmarks to watch for, and approximate distances. If the classmate will be taking a bus or subway, include all the information he or she will need to find your home.

Your directions will be scored according to this checklist. After writing your first draft, review the checklist and make any needed improvements. Then write your final draft.

You will earn your best score if:

☐   your paragraphs are written in a logical order.

☐   readers can easily understand your directions.

☐   you have included every necessary step and helpful piece of information.

☐   your directions are sequenced in a logical order.

☐   you have not included unimportant things that the reader does not need to know.

☐   you have not repeated information unnecessarily.

☐   you make no spelling, grammar, punctuation, or capitalization errors.

GO ➜

Plan Your Writing

Use these pages to plan your writing. The more planning you do now, the less revising you will have to do later. You might find this graphic organizer helpful.

```
┌──────────────────────────────────────┐
│                                      │
└──────────────────────────────────────┘
                   ▼
┌──────────────────────────────────────┐
│                                      │
└──────────────────────────────────────┘
                   ▼
┌──────────────────────────────────────┐
│                                      │
└──────────────────────────────────────┘
                   ▼
┌──────────────────────────────────────┐
│                                      │
└──────────────────────────────────────┘
                   ▼
┌──────────────────────────────────────┐
│                                      │
└──────────────────────────────────────┘
                   ▼
┌──────────────────────────────────────┐
│                                      │
└──────────────────────────────────────┘
                   ▼
┌──────────────────────────────────────┐
│                                      │
└──────────────────────────────────────┘
                   ▼
┌──────────────────────────────────────┐
│                                      │
└──────────────────────────────────────┘
```

GO ➡

Advantage Test Prep Grade 7 © 2005 Creative Teaching Press

Write Your First Draft

Use all the skills you have learned to write a first draft. Use an extra sheet of paper if necessary.

_____

_____

_____

_____

_____

_____

_____

_____

_____

_____

_____

_____

_____

_____

_____

_____

GO ➡

GO →

Advantage Test Prep Grade 7 © 2005 Creative Teaching Press

Write Your Final Draft

Now it's time to write your final draft. Use the writer's checklist on page 89 to make sure that you will achieve the best possible score. Carefully proofread your work when you are done.

_____

_____

_____

_____

_____

_____

_____

_____

_____

_____

_____

_____

_____

_____

GO ➡

_____

_____

_____

_____

_____

_____

_____

_____

_____

Give Yourself a Score

Go back to the scoring rubric on page 31. Use the rubric to score your work. Give yourself a score from 4 to 0 for each category. Then ask someone else to score your writing and compare the scores.

How I Scored It

Content and Ideas	Organization	Sentence Structure and Clarity	Spelling, Punctuation, Usage, and Grammar
_____	_____	_____	_____

How Someone Else Scored It

Content and Ideas	Organization	Sentence Structure and Clarity	Spelling, Punctuation, Usage, and Grammar
_____	_____	_____	_____

STOP

25 Which sentence contains an adjective?

- Ⓐ No one saw me enter the house.
- Ⓑ I crept very quietly up the stairs.
- Ⓒ Suddenly I heard a sound behind me.
- Ⓓ It was a strange moan, filling the darkness.

26 Choose the answer that best completes the sentence.

Until I receive _____ money, I will put her tickets on the top shelf.

- Ⓕ David's
- Ⓖ Alexandra's
- Ⓗ Mom and Dad's
- Ⓙ my next-door neighbors'

27 Which sentence correctly uses an infinitive?

- Ⓐ Does your sister like to golf?
- Ⓑ Let's go to the golf course today.
- Ⓒ Tomorrow may be too hot for golf.
- Ⓓ Swimming is a better choice when it's hot.

28 Which sentence is correct?

- Ⓕ Don't do that again, it's dangerous.
- Ⓖ I asked you Alicia to open the window.
- Ⓗ Before you answer the question, be sure to think about your answer.
- Ⓙ The game was close; but we won it with a touchdown in the last minute.

29 Which sentence is correct?

- Ⓐ Where did you get the shoes the green ones you wore to the party?
- Ⓑ We're going to California (how cool is that?) on vacation next summer.
- Ⓒ My mom repaired the toaster (because it was burning the bread to a cinder).
- Ⓓ Maria's older brother [Juan, not Eduardo] is going away to college in the fall.

GO →

30 Which sentence does NOT contain a pronoun?

- Ⓕ Her dog is a mixed breed.
- Ⓖ Should we play Clue or Monopoly?
- Ⓗ Paul passed the test, but Garth did not.
- Ⓙ Give Sanjit the ticket if you don't want to go to the game.

31 Which sentence is correct?

- Ⓐ We never did see no birds when we went bird-watching.
- Ⓑ When you pointed at a tree, I couldn't see nothing.
- Ⓒ None of us knew where to look for birds.
- Ⓓ Our guide wasn't no good.

32 Look at the underlined words. Which is spelled correctly?

- Ⓕ My sister's daughters are my <u>neices</u>.
- Ⓖ Sandra's little brother just had his <u>eighth</u> birthday.
- Ⓗ These pills are supposed to <u>releive</u> the pain of aching muscles.
- Ⓙ The new puppy got into a lot of <u>mischeif</u> when its owners went out.

33 Choose the sentence that uses correct punctuation and capitalization.

- Ⓐ my cousin Shana's favorite basketball team is the Boston Celtics
- Ⓑ My cousin Shana's favorite basketball team is the Boston Celtics?
- Ⓒ My Cousin Shana's favorite basketball team is the boston celtics.
- Ⓓ My cousin Shana's favorite basketball team is the Boston Celtics.

34 Which sentence is correct?

- Ⓕ Monica and Luis will sing on Friday, Lucinda and Rex will sing on Saturday.
- Ⓖ Monica and Luis will sing on Friday and, Lucinda and Rex will sing on Saturday.
- Ⓗ Monica and Luis will sing on Friday, and Lucinda and Rex will sing on Saturday.
- Ⓙ Monica and Luis will sing on Friday; and Lucinda and Rex will sing on Saturday.

GO →

Advantage Test Prep Grade 7 © 2005 Creative Teaching Press

35 Which of the following is a declarative sentence?

  Ⓐ   What a bad dog

  Ⓑ   That dog's name is Rosie

  Ⓒ   Get out of the flower bed, Rosie

  Ⓓ   Do you know how old Rosie is now

36 Which sentence correctly uses a gerund phrase?

  Ⓕ   An effective fund-raiser must enjoy asking people to donate money.

  Ⓖ   The governor is making a speech to the legislature tomorrow.

  Ⓗ   Speaking for myself, I don't care for kung-fu movies.

  Ⓙ   Jogging is good exercise.

37 Look at the underlined words. Which is spelled incorrectly?

  Ⓐ   If you want to <u>acheive</u> your goals, you'll need to work hard.

  Ⓑ   Do you know how a <u>piece</u> of apple pie got under your bed?

  Ⓒ   The doctor said he should reduce his <u>weight</u>.

  Ⓓ   That movie was so bad it's beyond <u>belief</u>!

38 Which sentence correctly uses a past participle?

  Ⓕ   Melissa lost the book borrowed from the library.

  Ⓖ   Our neighbor loaned us a chain saw to cut a tree branch.

  Ⓗ   Bart was having some trouble with the geography questions.

  Ⓙ   Thinking I was lost, the kind woman asked if I needed any help.

39 Choose the answer that best completes the sentence.

  Ayisha's mom and dad went to _____ 20th high school class reunion.

  Ⓐ   her

  Ⓑ   his

  Ⓒ   its

  Ⓓ   their

GO

40 Read the paragraph. Which sentence would make the best closing sentence?

Matthew Brady was one of the first photographers. He is best known for his photographs of the Civil War era. Risking his life, he led a team of assistants from battlefield to battle field. They carried their equipment in a kind of rolling photographic laboratory. His subjects ranged from wounded soldiers to Abraham Lincoln himself.

- Ⓕ Brady was almost killed at the Battle of Bull Run.
- Ⓖ Brady's assistants actually took many of the photos.
- Ⓗ Brady worked as a portrait photographer before the war began.
- Ⓙ Brady's photographs are a valuable source of information about the Civil War.

41 Which sentence does NOT contain a conjunction?

- Ⓐ You can either call me or e-mail me with your answer.
- Ⓑ The moon won't rise over the trees until about midnight.
- Ⓒ Dogs and cats are the most popular kinds of pets in our class.
- Ⓓ Sean said he would come to the meeting, but Tiffany can't make it.

42 Choose the option with the correct spelling to complete the sentence.

Brenda's remark about my jacket was _____ rude.

- Ⓕ totaly
- Ⓖ totally
- Ⓗ tottally
- Ⓙ totaley

43 Which sentence is correct?

- Ⓐ She didn't have no reason to push me.
- Ⓑ Nobody saw me enter the old building.
- Ⓒ We hadn't never seen a movie as good as that!
- Ⓓ I couldn't think of nothing to say when the teacher called on me.

44 Which sentence contains a pronoun?

- Ⓕ Jacie's scarf is on the table.
- Ⓖ When will the pizza arrive?
- Ⓗ Look at the horse tossing its mane!
- Ⓙ Whenever Martin finishes cutting the grass, Dad will fix dinner.

GO

45 Which of the following is a correct compound sentence?

- Ⓐ Snakes, lizards, and turtles are all reptiles.
- Ⓑ A boa constrictor uses its muscles to squeeze small animals.
- Ⓒ Have you ever seen a komodo dragon, there's one at the zoo?
- Ⓓ Some reptiles are quite small, but others, like alligators, can be huge.

46 Read the paragraph. Which sentence would make the best topic sentence?

It was carved by the Colorado River over a period of 6 million years. Its rock layers of many colors have amazed visitors. The canyon is so deep that different elevations have different climates. No one who has seen the sun set over Grand Canyon will ever forget the sight.

- Ⓕ Few natural wonders can match the Grand Canyon.
- Ⓖ The Grand Canyon became a national park in 1919.
- Ⓗ Explorer John Wesley Powell explored the canyon in 1869.
- Ⓙ The mighty Colorado River supplies water for thirsty Californians.

47 Choose the sentence that uses correct punctuation and capitalization.

- Ⓐ Dad bought the Turkish carpet at a store near the Empire State Building.
- Ⓑ Dad bought the Turkish carpet at a store near the empire state building.
- Ⓒ Dad bought the turkish carpet at a store near the Empire State Building
- Ⓓ dad bought the Turkish Carpet at a store near the Empire State building.

48 Which of the following is a declarative sentence?

- Ⓕ Watch out
- Ⓖ What's that sound
- Ⓗ What a gorgeous kitten
- Ⓙ I'll tell you a secret

49 Which of the following is an imperative sentence?

- Ⓐ Don't touch that
- Ⓑ Why shouldn't I
- Ⓒ It's so hot it will burn you
- Ⓓ Oh no, Julian touched the burner

GO ➡

50 Choose the option with the correct spelling to complete the sentence.

The _____ of that building helps it fit in with the other buildings on the block.

- Ⓕ plainess
- Ⓖ planness
- Ⓗ plainness
- Ⓙ plainnes

51 Which sentence correctly uses a gerund?
- Ⓐ JoEllen is lifting weights to get stronger.
- Ⓑ Some other people I know hate exercising.
- Ⓒ Maybe you're considering an exercise program, too.
- Ⓓ Thinking about how hard she works out, her friends admire her.

52 Choose the sentence that uses hyphenation correctly.
- Ⓕ The canned food drive is about one-half completed with a week left.
- Ⓖ Two-thirds of the club members have contributed to the fund.
- Ⓗ I'm grateful for these easy to understand instructions.
- Ⓙ Mia's sister is twenty two.

53 Choose the sentence in which the gerund phrase is correctly underlined.
- Ⓐ I'm one of those people <u>who really enjoys going to the barber</u>.
- Ⓑ <u>Talking on a cell phone in a restaurant</u> is very bad manners.
- Ⓒ <u>Calling your grandfather right now is a terrific idea</u>.
- Ⓓ <u>Our chances of winning</u> the game are good.

54 Which of the following is NOT a compound sentence?
- Ⓕ Some people prefer apples; others like oranges.
- Ⓖ My sister likes apples, but my brother is a pear fan.
- Ⓗ Citrus fruits include oranges, lemons, limes, and grapefruits.
- Ⓙ Berries are a kind of fruit, and I love raspberries and strawberries.

STOP

55 $6^2 = $ _____

    Ⓐ   8   Ⓒ   36

    Ⓑ   12   Ⓓ   216

56 A box of 12 mechanical pencils from Business World costs $10.30. The same box at Office Giant costs $11.62. How much will Michael save on each pencil if he buys them at Business World?

    Ⓕ $1.32

    Ⓖ $1.10

    Ⓗ   32 cents

    Ⓙ   11 cents

57 Which group of numbers is written in order from least to greatest?

    Ⓐ   8,832;   8,823;   8,238

    Ⓑ   52,192;   52,219;   52,921

    Ⓒ   954,090;   954,009;   945,900

    Ⓓ   4,976,580;   4,679, 850;   4,670,968

58 A bar graph shows the number of goals each member of the soccer team has scored over one season. Which of the following statements is true about the bar graph?

    Ⓕ   The smallest bar will represent the number of players who scored one goal.

    Ⓖ   The largest bar will represent the number of goals scored by the whole team.

    Ⓗ   The largest bar will represent the highest number of goals scored by one player.

    Ⓙ   The largest bar will represent the number of players who scored a goal in every game.

59 $7 \times (-3) = $ _____

    Ⓐ   4

    Ⓑ   -4

    Ⓒ   21

    Ⓓ   -21

GO

60 Marisa wants to buy a softball mitt that costs $81. She has saved up $36. What percentage of the total cost does she still have to save?

- Ⓕ 36%
- Ⓖ 45%
- Ⓗ 56%
- Ⓙ 65%

61 What is the area of the shaded figure?

- Ⓐ 7 1/2 square units
- Ⓑ 8 1/2 square units
- Ⓒ 9 1/2 square units
- Ⓓ 11 square units

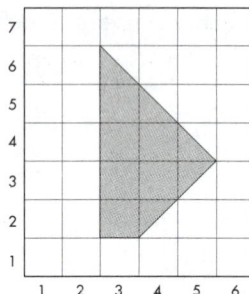

62 3/4 – 1/3 = _____

- Ⓕ 5/12
- Ⓖ 7/12
- Ⓗ 2/4
- Ⓙ 2/3

63 What is the volume of this solid?

- Ⓐ 32 cm³
- Ⓑ 120 cm³
- Ⓒ 1,080 cm³
- Ⓓ 1,800 cm³

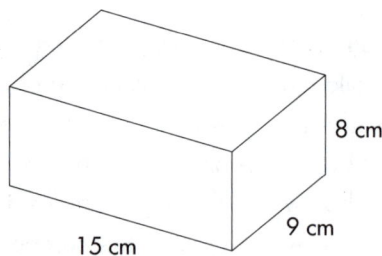

8 cm

9 cm

15 cm

64 Rewrite the ratios $n : 5$ and $16 : 40$ as a proportion and solve for the missing number.

- Ⓕ 1
- Ⓖ 2
- Ⓗ 3
- Ⓙ 4

GO

65 $6.7 \times 10^6 =$

  (A) 67,000

  (B) 670,000

  (C) 6,700,000

  (D) 67,000,000

66 During a six-week period, the school aluminum can drive collected 102, 92, 136, 174, 90, and 168 aluminum cans weekly. What was the range of the number of cans collected weekly?

  (F) 174

  (G) 127

  (H) 90

  (J) 84

67 The prime factorization of 72 is

  (A) $3^2 \times 2^3$

  (B) $3^3 \times 2^2$

  (C) $3^2 \times 4^3$

  (D) 3^5

68 Look at this spinner to the right. What is the probability that you will spin a hockey puck, then a basketball?

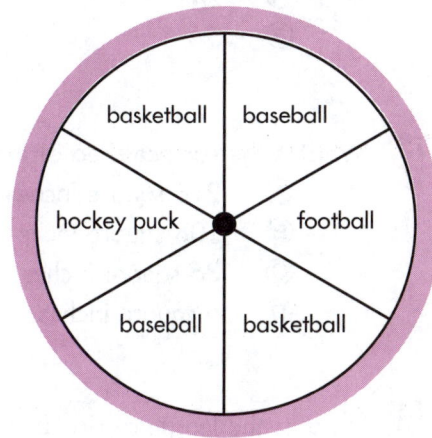

  (F) 1/3

  (G) 1/6

  (H) 1/18

  (J) 1/36

basketball baseball

hockey puck football

baseball basketball

69 Which number correctly completes the proportion?
$5/8 = 15/n$

  (A) 16

  (B) 20

  (C) 24

  (D) 28

GO

70 0.71 ÷ 6.5 = _____
- Ⓕ 0.1092
- Ⓖ 1.092
- Ⓗ 10.92
- Ⓙ 109.20

71 Which equation does the graph show?
- Ⓐ $x = 2y$
- Ⓑ $x = y - 1$
- Ⓒ $x - 1 = y$
- Ⓓ $2x = y$

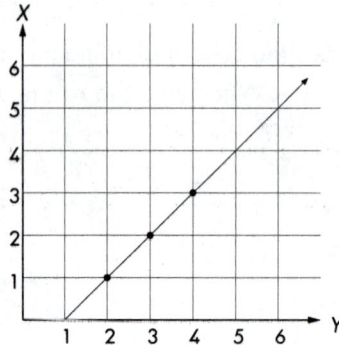

72 $\sqrt{64}$ = _____
- Ⓕ 16
- Ⓖ 8
- Ⓗ 24
- Ⓙ 54

73 What is the surface area of this solid?
- Ⓐ 216 square inches
- Ⓑ 108 square inches
- Ⓒ 36 square inches
- Ⓓ 6 square inches

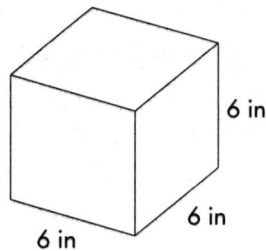

6 in

6 in

6 in

74 What is the length of side *b* in this triangle?
- Ⓕ 32 in
- Ⓖ 24 in
- Ⓗ 16 in
- Ⓙ 8 in

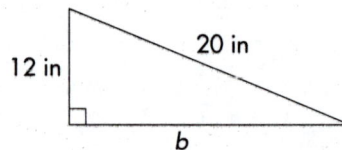

12 in

20 in

b

GO

75 Jared and his friends sold granola bars to support the school band. Jared sold 32 bars, while his friends sold 36, 26, 21, 18, and 25 bars. What is the mean number of bars sold by all, rounded to the nearest whole number?

- (A) 18
- (B) 21
- (C) 26
- (D) 27

76 What is the area of the shaded figure?

- (F) 9 1/2 square units
- (G) 10 1/2 square units
- (H) 11 1/2 square units
- (J) 13 square units

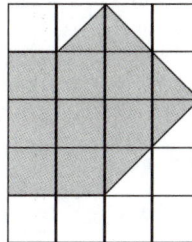

77 Solve for the variable y in the equation $4y = 32$.

- (A) 5
- (B) 6
- (C) 7
- (D) 8

78 Which graph shows the equation $x \div 2 = y$?

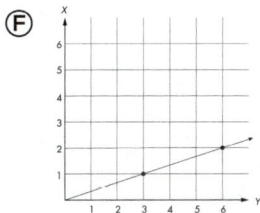

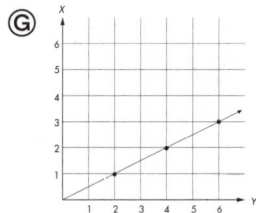

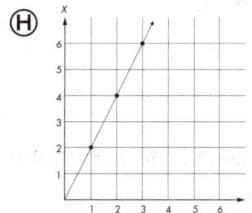

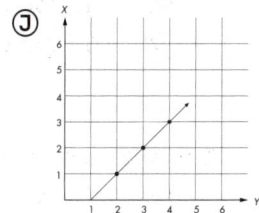

(F)   (G)   (H)   (J)

79 What is the length of side c in this triangle?

- (A) 900 cm
- (B) 90 cm
- (C) 42 cm
- (D) 30 cm

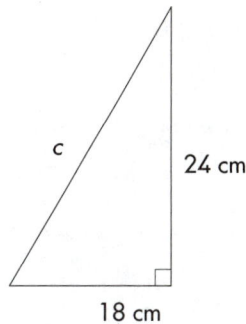

c

24 cm

18 cm

GO

80 Which equation does NOT have a solution of 7?

    Ⓕ $3x = 21$

    Ⓖ $18 \div 2 = x$

    Ⓗ $x - 3 = 4$

    Ⓙ $2 + x = 9$

81 Which pair of figures is NOT congruent?

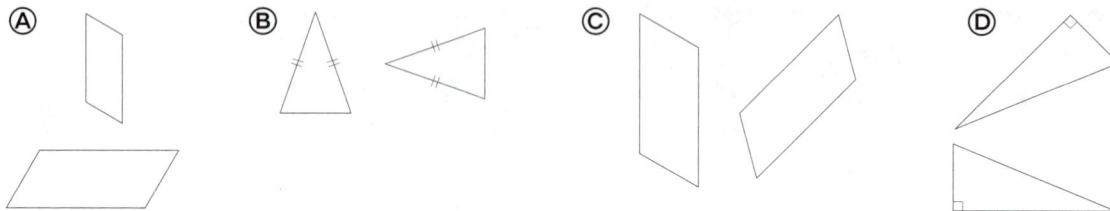

  Ⓐ   Ⓑ   Ⓒ   Ⓓ

82 $3^2 \times 5^3$ is the prime factorization of _____.

    Ⓕ   1,696

    Ⓖ   1,125

    Ⓗ   325

    Ⓙ   15

83 The product of 79 x 4.93 is about _____.

    Ⓐ   4000

    Ⓑ   400

    Ⓒ   40

    Ⓓ   4.0

84 If this shape is flipped across line *EF*, what will it look like?

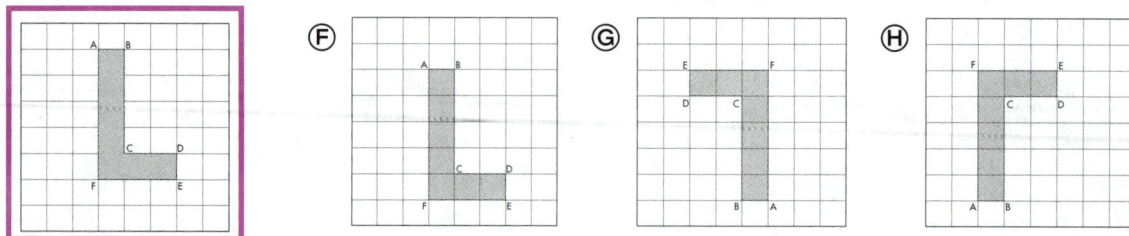

    Ⓕ   Ⓖ   Ⓗ

GO

85 What is the value of the expression $2n + 3$ if $n = 6$?

    Ⓐ   5

    Ⓑ   11

    Ⓒ   15

    Ⓓ   23

86 4 is the greatest common factor of _____.

    Ⓕ   8 and 24

    Ⓖ   12 and 3

    Ⓗ   12 and 18

    Ⓙ   12 and 16

87 $1/5 + 2/7 =$ _____

    Ⓐ   17/35

    Ⓑ   3/10

    Ⓒ   3/5

    Ⓓ   3/7

88 Estimate an answer for this division problem: $8{,}102 \div 422$.

    Ⓕ   2

    Ⓖ   20

    Ⓗ   200

    Ⓙ   2000

89 The greatest common factor of 72 and 90 is _____.

    Ⓐ   8

    Ⓑ   9

    Ⓒ   15

    Ⓓ   18

GO

90 $1.8 \times 10^4 =$ _____

  Ⓕ 180 Ⓗ 18,000
  Ⓖ 1800 Ⓙ 180,000

91 If this shape is turned on point *B* 180° counter-clockwise, what will it look like?

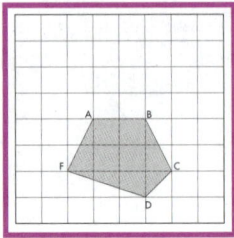

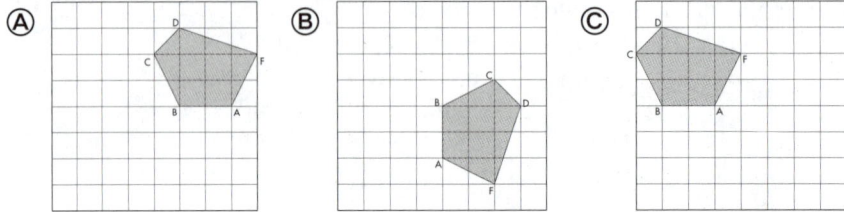

92 These figures are congruent. Which angle corresponds to angle *C*?

  Ⓕ angle W
  Ⓖ angle X
  Ⓗ angle Y
  Ⓕ angle Z

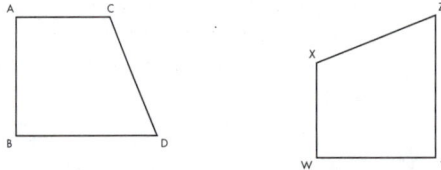

93 Sam has six identical marbles in his pocket. They are red, yellow, white, green, blue, and brown. What is the probability that he can pull a white one and then a green one out of his pocket, if he puts the white one back in his pocket after he pulls it?

  Ⓐ 1/36 Ⓒ 2/6
  Ⓑ 2/36 Ⓓ 1/6

94 Look at this bar graph. It shows the number of students in a class with different kinds of pets. Nine students had cats, eight had dogs, four had reptiles, four had fish, and two had birds. Which bars represent dogs and birds?

  Ⓕ 3 and 5
  Ⓖ 3 and 4
  Ⓗ 1 and 2
  Ⓙ 2 and 5

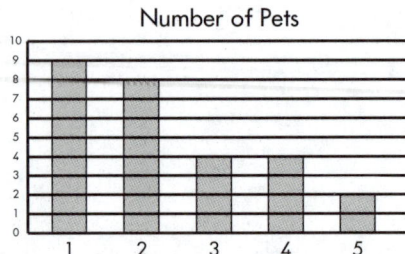

Number of Pets

STOP

Advantage Test Prep Grade 7 © 2005 Creative Teaching Press

Reading

Page 8
The correct answer is option J. The paragraph is describing the effect of thrust that keeps a plane or bird flying through the air. The context tells you that the word *aloft* means "up in the air or in the sky."

Page 9
The correct answer is option J. The word *beneficiaries* shares a root with the word *benefit*. A benefit is something good or positive. Modern business travelers have benefited from Bernoulli's ideas because they can travel great distances easily and speedily by jet plane.

Page 10
The correct answer is option J. The cause, Bernoulli's discoveries about the science of flight, had as its effect the eventual development of airplanes based on his discoveries. The other choices are not effects, or results, of Bernoulli's discoveries.

Page 11
Option H is correct. Options G and F are steps that are taken after cutting the strip of paper. Option J is not a step in the procedure.

Page 12
Option F is not supported by the selection. Air pressure is well understood. The other generalizations are logical statements that are supported by the selection.

Page 14
All four choices are meanings of the word *grave*, but only option J is correct. Because *grave* in the sentence modifies a noun, *voice*, it has to be an adjective. That eliminates option F, a noun. Options G and H are adjectives, but they do not fit the meaning of the sentence as well as *serious*.

Page 15
Option J is correct. A building is designed, as a symphony is composed. *Building* and *symphony* are nouns. In option G, the noun *bridge* does not make sense with the verb *compose* because a bridge is built, not composed. Option F is incorrect because *create* is a verb. Option H is incorrect because *wonderful* is an adjective.

Page 16
Option F is correct. As the boy's father, Daedalus certainly knew what kind of personality Icarus had. He felt he had to give the boy a special warning so that he would not get carried away and meet a terrible fate.

Page 17
Option G is correct. This is an event that took place before the story begins, but it is still an important plot event. The correct order of the plot events listed as choices is G, H, J, F.

Page 18
Option G is the correct answer. The conflict between the father and son is based on their different personalities: Daedalus is wiser and more cautious, while Icarus is younger and more reckless.

Page 19
Option G is correct. There is nothing in the story, or in most readers' experiences, to suggest that it was wrong to seek freedom for himself and Icarus. The other options are all supported by the text and by readers' knowledge, judgment, and own experiences.

Page 20
Option H is correct. The hint the author gives is the word *seemed*; yes, their situation seems hopeless, but Daedalus is a great inventor and may eventually think of something. That is exactly what happens. The other choices do not foreshadow events to come later in the story.

Page 22
The symbol is the barren field frozen with snow. It is a good symbol of a life in which dreams have died because a barren field can grow no crops. The snow adds to the chilly feeling of loss and unhappiness in a life without dreams.

Page 23
Like almost everyone, Hughes probably experienced for himself the heartbreak of broken dreams. He probably also had others tell him about their broken dreams and how their loss made them feel.

Page 24
Option G is correct. The distance from Las Cruces to the airport is about 50 miles. Because it is a round trip, you need to double this distance.

Page 25
The number of takeoffs and landings is greatest in the morning, possibly because business travelers are flying out, drops off during the day, and then picks up around dinner time.

Page 26
Option G is correct. In this problem, you first need to find half of the total number of votes of 256: 256 ÷ 2 = 128. Then find the two names, the sum of which equals 128. A quick way to eliminate choices is to look at the left-most digits. Because the total you're looking for is 128, the sum of the two digits in the ones column must equal 8. That limits your choices to names with totals ending in 1 or 7. Adding the totals for Eagles and Falcons results in a total of 128.

Page 27
Option F is correct. A careful reading of the dates tells that these events took place only one year apart. You can also tell this by how close together they are on the time line.

Page 28

Option J is correct. You can tell from the index entries that each of the other options is too limited to be the title of the book.

Page 29

Here's a possible answer: The Greek roots mean "sphere that turns or changes," and the troposphere is the where most of earth's weather phenomena take place.

Language

Page 41

The correct answer is G. *Dad*, the first word in the sentence, and *Egyptian*, a proper adjective, are capitalized. The sentence ends with a period. In option F, *egyptian* should be capitalized. *History museum* is not a proper noun and should not be capitalized. In option H, *dad* should have a capital letter, while *Mummy* should not be capitalized because it is not a proper noun. Option J is not a question, so it should not end with a question mark. *Egyptian* should be capitalized.

Page 42

Option G is correct. *Mean-sounding* is a single adjective. In option F, *three fourths* is used as a modifier, so it should have a hyphen. In option H, there should be a hyphen between *seventy* and *five*. In option J, *hard to see* should be joined by hyphens—the words make up one adjective.

Page 43

Option F is correct. The words *eighty-seven* are extra material inserted in the original quotation. In option G, there should be parentheses, not brackets, because *do not confuse it with the brown tube* is apart from the meaning of the sentence and it is not a quotation from another writer. In option H, the parentheses should enclose *I like the blue one best*, not *Have you decided which shirt*. In option J, the phrase *next to the park* should not be in parentheses because it is a necessary part of the sentence.

Page 44

Option H is correct. The comma is used to set off a dependent clause when it begins a sentence. Option F requires a semicolon to join the two independent clauses. In option G, *Mr. Thomas* is an interruption in the sentence and should be set off by commas. Option J needs a comma before the conjunction *and*, not a semicolon.

Page 45

The correct choice is option F. The past participle is *Baked*, modifying *parking lot*. In option G, *feeling* is a present participle. In option H, *baked* is the past tense of the verb *bake*. In option J, *feeling* is the present progressive tense of the verb *feel*.

Page 46

Option F is correct. The words *telling people about his trips* is a gerund phrase used as the direct object. In option G, *traveling* is used as a gerund, but because it does not include modifiers, it is not a gerund phrase. In option H, *is planning* is the verb. In option J, *listening* is a present participle that modifies *I'd*.

Page 47

The correct answer is option F. It agrees in number (David and Sam are two people) with the plural pronoun *they*. Each of the other options is singular.

Page 48

The correct answer is option H. The word *to* is used as part of the infinitive *to play*. In option F, *toward* is a preposition. In option G, *on* is a preposition. In option J, *under* is a preposition.

Page 49

The correct answer is option J. It expresses a request; therefore, it is imperative.

Page 50

The correct answer is option F. It is a simple sentence with a compound subject, *Lewis and Clark*. All the others are compound sentences joined by conjunctions.

Page 51

The correct choice is option G. It contains only one negative word, *not*. In option F, *isn't* and *nothing* make a double negative. In option H, *haven't* and *nothing* make a double negative. In option J, *didn't* and *no* make a double negative.

Page 52

Option H is correct. Because the paragraph discusses reasons for NASCAR's popularity, the correct closing sentence makes a prediction about the sport's future popularity. The other answers are details about stock car racing.

Page 53

The correct answer is option G. The *y* in *carry* is changed to an *i* before adding the *-ed* ending.

Page 54

The correct answer is option G. The sound in *veil* is *a*, like in *neighbor* and *weigh*. The other options should be spelled with an *ie* combination.

Mathematics

Page 56
The correct answer is option F. Comparing digits from the left, you find that the 1 in 5,762,410 is less than the 5 in 5,762,450. All the other options are less than 5,762,410.

Page 57
The correct answer is option G. Multiplying 3.4 times 10 six times gives an answer of 3 million, 4 hundred thousand.

Page 58
The correct answer is option H. The number multiplied by itself once that equals 81 is 9.

Page 59
The correct answer is option F. The LCD for 3 and 5 is 15. Multiply the numerator and denominator of 1/5 by 3 and the numerator and denominator of 1/3 by 5 to get fractions with like denominators of 15 (12/15 and 5/15). Then subtract the numerators to get 7/15.

Page 60
The product of 4 and 5 is 20. Because the product of two numbers with different signs is a negative number, option J is correct.

Page 61
The correct answer is option J. Moving the decimal point in both dividend and the divisor makes the problem $44 \div 920 = 0.0478$.

Page 62
The correct answer is option H. You can use compatible numbers by looking at the first digit in each number. Because the first digit of the divisor is 3, think of the basic facts for 3. Then, because $3 \times 3 = 9$, use 9,000 as a compatible number for 9,016 and 30 for a compatible number for 31. $9,000 \div 30 = 300$.

Page 63
The correct answer is option G. The factors of 12 are 1, 2, 3, 4, 6, and 12. The factors of 30 are 1, 2, 3, 5, 6, 10, 15, and 30. The GCF is 6. The GCF for option F (8 and 12) is 4. The GCF for option H (12 and 36) is 12. The GCF for option J (24 and 56) is 8.

Page 64
Option J is the correct answer. $2^3 = 2 \times 2 \times 2 = 8$. $5^2 = 5 \times 5 = 25$. $8 \times 25 = 200$.

Page 65
The correct answer is option F. Count up the number of completely shaded units (3) and the number of half-shaded units (9). The half-shaded units add up to 4.5 square units. Add the totals together to get 7.5 square units as the area.

Page 66
The correct answer option J. The formula for finding the volume of a cube is $V = s^3$, or $V = 72^3$, or $72 \times 72 \times 72 = 373,348$ cubic centimeters.

Page 67
Option H is the correct answer. To find it you must find the area of each of the rectangles that make up the outside surface of the solid. There are two sides that are 3 cm by 6 cm, two that are 10 cm by 6 cm, and two that are 3 cm by 10 cm. This creates two sides with an area of 18 cm^2 each, two with an area of 60 cm^2 each, and two with an area of 30 cm^2 each. The sum of the areas of these six sides is 216 cm^2.

Page 68
The correct answer is option G. Use the lengths of the two sides given to rewrite the equation as $9^2 + b^2 = 15^2$, or $81 + b^2 = 225$. Subtract 81 from 225 to get 144, which equals b^2. The square root of 144 is 12, which is the length of side b.

Page 69
Option H is correct. Because angle C is an obtuse angle, you must find the only obtuse angle in the second figure, which is angle Y.

Page 70
The correct answer is option F. It has been flipped along line AJ. Option G has been slid along line AJ. Option H has flipped along lines BC and FG. Option J has been slid along lines AJ and AB.

Page 71
The correct answer is option J. Replace both n variables with the value 5 to get $3(5) + 4(5) = 15 + 20 = 35$.

Page 72
The correct answer is option J. Plug the value 12 into each equation. The variable in option H equals 14. The variable equals 12 in the other three choices.

Page 73
The correct answer is option F. Option G shows the graph of the equation $2x = y$. Option H shows the graph of the equation $x = y - 1$. Option J shows the graph of the equation $x \div 2 = y$.

Page 74
The correct answer is option J. The range is the difference between the greatest and least value in the data set. Subtract the lowest temperature, 52, from the highest, 69, to get 17. Option F is the greatest value. Option G is the mean. Option H is the mode.

Page 75
The correct answer is option F. The probability that you will spin a dog on the first spin is 2/4 (because two of the four sections are dogs), or 1/2. The chances that you will spin a cat on the second spin is 1/4. Multiplying the two fractions gives you a 1/8 chance of spinning a dog and then a cat.

Page 76

The correct answer is option F. Bar graphs show the relationship of different amounts, numbers, or values. The largest bar will show the test grade that the largest number of class members received on the test.

Page 77

The correct answer is option H. First you need to determine the price of a dozen (12) cans without the discount: multiply $23.55 \times 12 = $282.60. Then subtract the discounted price for 12 cans from this amount: $282.60 − $235.16 = $47.44. $47.44 is the amount she saved by buying 12 cans. To find the percentage this amount is of the original, non-discounted price, divide it by the original price: $47.44 ÷ $282.60 = 17%.

Page 78

The correct answer is option J. Rewrite the proportion as $2/n = 40 ÷ 100$. Using cross products, $40 \times n = 2 \times 100 = 200$, or $40n = 200$. Divide each side by 40 to isolate the variable on one side. This leaves $n = 5$. The missing number in the proportion is 5: $2 ÷ 5 = 40 ÷ 100$.

Practice Test: Reading

1 C
2 G
3 D
4 The correct order, as they would appear on a time line is Montgolfiers watch bits of paper float up the factory chimney; the brothers conclude that an unknown gas makes bags rise; the French king asks them to launch a balloon from his palace; they send animals up in a balloon; Benjamin Franklin watches their demonstration flight.

5 C
6 H
7 A
8 G
9 D
10 You should choose a map or a time line. A map would be useful to show the directions, locations, and distances of their balloon flights. A time line would be useful to show the chronological order of the events described in the selection. The other options would not be useful.
11 D
12 H
13 B
14 J
15 B
16 G
17 A
18 J
19 A
20 F
21 B
22 J
23 D
24 G

Practice Test: Language

25 D
26 G
27 A
28 H
29 B
30 H
31 C
32 G
33 D
34 H
35 B
36 F
37 A
38 G
39 D
40 J
41 B
42 G
43 B
44 H

45 D
46 F
47 A
48 J
49 A
50 H
51 B
52 F
53 B
54 H

Practice Test: Math

55 C
56 J
57 B
58 H
59 D
60 H
61 B
62 F
63 C
64 G
65 C
66 J
67 A
68 H
69 C
70 F
71 C
72 G
73 A
74 H
75 C
76 G
77 D
78 G
79 D
80 G
81 A
82 G
83 B
84 H
85 C
86 J
87 A
88 G
89 D
90 H
91 A
92 G
93 A
94 J